Kevin Brown *and* Annette Presley

THE LIBERATION DIET

Setting America Free from the Bondage of Health Misinformation!

Table *of* Contents

Disclaimer

The authors do not directly or indirectly dispense medical advice or prescribe the use of diet as a form of treatment for sickness without medical approval. Nutritionists and other experts in the field of health and nutrition hold widely varying views. It is not the intent of the authors to diagnose or prescribe. The intent is only to offer health information to help you cooperate with your health-care provider in your mutual quest for health. In the event you use this information without your health-care provider's approval, you are prescribing for yourself, which is your constitutional right, but the publisher and author assume no responsibility.

Foreword

As a physician, I was supposed to know the safest and most efficient way to lose weight and improve health. Yet when I decided to get my own body back into shape, my fifteen years of medical training as a family physician left me ill-equipped to achieve weight loss and meet exercise goals with a 100-hour per week work schedule. I needed professional help.

The solution was to find a personal trainer who would come to me on a flexible schedule and teach me about nutrition, dieting, and exercise. To minimize the risk for injuries, I also needed a trainer who would guide me through a routine one-on-one. I found that trainer in Kevin Brown, president of Visionary Trainers.

Before working with Kevin, I spent about six weeks on a poorly designed exercise program that was devoid of good nutritional and dieting advice. With twenty years experience as a personal trainer, Kevin had the expertise to develop a plan that had me eating better and exercising smarter, leading to a sixteen-pound weight loss in just four weeks. Now, Kevin and his co-author, Annette Presley, have written a book, *The Liberation Diet,* that tells the truth about the misinformation on weight management handed out by the diet industry and teaches us how to achieve lasting weight-loss success.

How does this book differ from the plethora of diet books out there? It's a revolutionary look at why conventional diets don't work and what we really should be eating to lose weight and stay healthy. Most weight-loss programs are monolithic in their approach, placing all individuals on the same regimen regardless of individual needs. Few people will achieve their weight-loss goals following the latest diet craze or hip exercise program, because they are only temporary solutions to a long-term problem. *The Liberation Diet* is a way of life that teaches you how to combine the right balance of nutrients, whole foods, and exercise to achieve permanent weight loss and a healthy life.

This book is groundbreaking work and a must read for both novice and advance trainees. I highly encourage anyone interested in safe, effective and drug-free weight loss to read *The Liberation Diet*. The experience will set you free to discover the secrets that will greatly improve your quality of life.

Dr. Woody Jackson, M.D.

Dr. Jackson is a board certified family practitioner and the head of Oxford Medical Associates in Oxford, Pennsylvania.

Introduction

Are you in?

For those readers who didn't see the movie *The Matrix*, Keanu Reeves was given a choice between a blue pill and a red pill. If he took the blue pill, life would go on as it always had; however, if he took the red pill, he would know the truth and leave the matrix. We aren't going to give you a pill, but we are going to share some very valuable truths so you can come out of the matrix, free to enjoy a healthier life.

So, what is the matrix? In the movie, the matrix was a computer-controlled environment where people thought they were living a normal life. In actuality, computers ruled the world and used human beings, hooked up to tubes in an incubator, as a source of energy. By getting a manipulated perception of what reality was, the people couldn't see that they were being controlled by the matrix.

Our matrix is set in twenty-first-century America and is a vast web of diet and healthcare industries, educational programs, government agencies, and media outlets, which are to some degree influenced by the large food and drug corporations. We are told *what's good for you is bad, and what's bad for you is good*. In our matrix, we are indoctrinated into the low-fat cult. We are told we should eat more grains, fruits and vegetables; we should limit red meats and fats; skim milk is touted as better than whole milk; and margarine is better than butter. Most of our foods come in a box, can, or package with ingredients that are manufactured in a laboratory instead of grown with love in a garden. These ingredients are given names that are so foreign to our language we cannot pronounce them, let alone classify them as plant, mineral, or animal. In today's matrix, we are told to *choke down eight glasses of water* a day to wash down all the fiber we are supposed to eat. Our salads suffer with fat-free dressing, and our taste buds are forced to live without salt. "All natural" is a creative term used to describe food that has had all the life-giving nutrients sucked right out of it. The pharmaceutical industry is busy inventing new diseases so they can push ever-increasing and more costly medication on healthy people. The FDA covers its eyes as the food industry adds toxic ingredients to canned, boxed, and packaged foods without alerting consumers to the health risks. We are forced to spend hours in the gym, slaving away at some machine, just to achieve a decent weight, yet we don't have time to prepare decent food.

Do we really want to live to a ripe old age if we have to *spend our last days in a nursing home?* Do we want our existence consisting of going from illness to illness? There just has to be something better than bland, tasteless food that doesn't satisfy our bodies or nourish our souls. There must be some alternative to medications and medical procedures that take away our freedom to live independently and enjoy all the things life has to offer.

Both Kevin and Annette (the authors) began their careers in the 1990s with great excitement. They were motivated to help people achieve good health and maintain normal weight, but soon found themselves struggling between what they were taught would help people and what was actually happening.

Annette spent most of her career in a hospital setting. She saw firsthand the financial, physical, and emotional toll obesity and disease took on her patients and was determined never to end up in a hospital or nursing home.

Following her own program, Annette began to eat the so-called healthy, low-fat diet. *She soon discovered that she was gaining weight rather than losing it.* In 2002, she experienced extreme emotional stress, which resulted in severe allergies that progressed into asthma. She could not walk a quarter of a mile without coughing up from her lungs, so she did what every American does. She went to the doctor and received a nebulizer, several different asthma medications, and prednisone. She faithfully filled the prescriptions, but dreaded taking the prednisone. As a dietitian, Annette was very aware of the side effects. She wanted another option, but it was clear she wasn't going to get it from the mainstream healthcare industry.

Here she was a registered dietitian, an expert on food and nutrition with a degree from an accredited university. She should know of something that could reverse her asthma, but she hadn't been taught that in school. Annette was taught that people didn't need vitamins; as long as you ate your six-to-eleven servings of grains and five servings of fruits and vegetables every day, you would get everything you needed from food.

Annette went outside her education, changed her diet, and added some nutritional supplements. *Within two weeks, she was able to stop breathing treatments and was able to start exercising again after six months*. She never did take the prednisone.

This was the genesis of Annette's journey into research that questioned her beliefs in a system that was clearly flawed. Through trial and error she began to discover that much of what she had been taught in school was wrong. The advice she was taught to hand out was *actually causing obesity and chronic disease*!

Annette had to choose between the red pill and the blue pill. She could take the blue pill, play along with the status quo, continue to preach the low-fat, high-carb dogma, and go on with life as normal; or she could take the red pill, start preaching the truth, and lead others out of the matrix to the real world where they would be liberated from obesity, disease, and medication. Putting her career at risk, she chose liberation.

Kevin's story is similar. He was in the world of personal training, gyms, treadmills, aerobic classes, and positive motivation. Sure, diet was important, but the only way to lose weight, or so he thought, was to exercise vigorously at least five or six days a week. Personal training is a *results-oriented business*, so in order to be successful, your clients need to lose weight. After a while, Kevin began to notice how difficult it was for people to lose weight on a low-fat, low-calorie diet even if they exercised seven days a week. This was especially true for women who were getting a little older with metabolisms that were getting a little slower. Some were *working very hard and barely making any progress*, which was frustrating to both Kevin and his clients. Similar to Annette, Kevin noticed that he was also one of those people having difficulty keeping his weight down. Kevin knew what he was doing, or at least thought he did. He believed he had acquired the key to health and weight loss; but the key didn't fit.

Throughout the years, Kevin attended continuing education seminars and noticed the same message being preached: "Never recommend vitamins and minerals to your clients," and "Never use a low-carbohydrate diet." *Why was everyone so against vitamins and so in love with carbohydrates?* As Kevin learned about different diet programs, several of which seemed a little bizarre, it seemed odd that everything was okay in moderation except vitamins and low-carb diets. In one class, the instructor encouraged personal trainers to recommend steroids to their clients, but Kevin couldn't even think of a situation where he would put a client on steroids. Kevin decided that vitamins would be better than steroids, so he began to use whole-food supplements on himself and his clients with great results. That set him on the path to discovery.

Since he experienced good results from "taboo" supplements, Kevin decided to try the low-carb diet. After one week of eating mostly protein and fat (most of it saturated fat), *Kevin's excess weight was flying off and he felt twenty years younger!* He began to use the low-carb diet on his clients, and they also experienced amazing weight loss and better health. *The very things Kevin was warned against were the things that helped his clients the most.* Kevin could no longer trust the information he was taught, so he set out to find out why this misinformation was being propagated. Kevin chose the red pill.

Through many years of research, Annette and Kevin have now developed a lifestyle diet system that has improved the lives of many people, often with dramatic results. Their clients enjoy better health, permanent weight loss, more energy, more stamina, and the freedom to enjoy life to the fullest. This book is your key to be liberated from the old matrix to enter a new and exciting world where you will experience freedom from chronic disease and obesity to live a full and abundant life.

The Rise of Fake Food and Misinformation

What do candles, soap, and buttermilk biscuits have in common?
Industrial waste.

It all started back in 1837 when William Proctor and his brother-in-law James Gamble combined their candle- and soap-making businesses to make it easier to obtain the beef tallow and lard necessary for their products. Tallow and lard were hard to come by because of fierce competition and price fixing. Irritated at having to pay high prices that cut into their profit margin for their raw ingredients, Proctor and Gamble began to search for an alternative to tallow and lard.

The boys invested in cottonseed mills. Before cotton can be incorporated into a T-shirt or Q-tip, the seeds are removed and discarded as industrial waste. Proctor and Gamble discovered that oil could be extracted from these seeds. Unfortunately, the oil was unstable and not very useful for their products, but, in 1907, with the help of the German chemist E.C. Kayser, Proctor and Gamble developed the science of hydrogenation. They took the cottonseed oil and added hydrogen molecules combined with extreme heat and pressure, creating a solid, stable form of cottonseed oil that happened to look a lot like lard.

Turning industrial waste into food

This new product worked fairly well for soap and candles, but the candle business was dwindling due to the invention of the light bulb.

Candles were used for light back in those days, not for fragrance or decoration, so with demand decreasing, Proctor and Gamble had to find some other use for all the solid cottonseed oil they were producing. The conversation went something like this: "Well, it looks like lard and acts like lard. Say, why don't we stick it in a can and call it a food?!" So they stuck the stuff in a can, called it Crisco, short for "crystallized cottonseed oil," and put it on the market in 1911 as an alternative to lard.

But how do you convince housewives that an industrial waste product is safe to eat?

Proctor and Gamble launched the most ingenious advertising campaign ever. First, they wiped out the competition, lard and butter, with the statement "more economical than butter and healthier than animal fats." The boys didn't bother to do any studies comparing the health benefits of Crisco to animal fats; they just said what they needed to say to sell their product. Second, they published a cookbook with 615 recipes all calling for Crisco. The cookbook taught housewives how to use this new fangled fat and appealed to their sense of pride with pictures of young women teaching their mothers and grandmothers to use Crisco instead of animal fats. Crisco was advertised in the cookbook as cleaner than and more easily digestible than animal fats, and children growing up on Crisco would be well-behaved and intelligent. Crisco was the choice for any enlightened, modern mother who cared about the cleanliness of her home, her standing in the community, and the behavior and health of her children. Jewish housewives embraced Crisco with open arms because it behaved like butter but could be eaten with meat and was marketed as such. Another assumed benefit of Crisco was its two-year shelf life, which ensured that consumers would be able to use the entire can before it went bad. Crisco became a household staple and the first truly fake food.

The formula was brilliant; take an industrial waste product, put it in a can, and market it as a health food.

Crisco became the first in a long line of fake foods that have replaced real food in the American diet. Following close on the heels of Crisco is soy lecithin, the industrial waste product of soybean oil. Lecithin, or phosphatidylcholine, is a component of all cell membranes allowing both water soluble and fat soluble substances to pass through. Oil and water don't mix, but if you add an egg yolk, they can be combined. Lecithin is just like the egg yolk. Without it, water soluble substances such as vitamin C would not be able to enter cells. Egg yolk happens to be one of the best sources of lecithin in the diet. You may remember that lecithin was a very popular health supplement in the 1970s.

Soy lecithin is the sludge left over from the processing of soybean oil. Kaayla T. Daniel describes this sludge in her book, *The Whole Soy Story*, as follows: "It is a waste product containing residues of solvents and pesticides and has a consistency ranging from a gummy fluid to a plastic solid. The color of lecithin ranges from a dirty tan to reddish brown. Manufacturers therefore subject lecithin to a bleaching process to turn it into a more appealing light yellow hue. The hexane extraction process commonly used in soybean oil manufacture today yields less lecithin than the older ethanol-benzol process, but produces a more marketable lecithin with better color, reduced odor and less bitter flavor."

Soybean oil is the most common vegetable oil used today, and manufacturers need a cheap way to get rid of the industrial waste left behind. In the 1930s, manufacturers hired scientists to invent ways to use the sludge left over from soybean oil. The scientists discovered over 1,000 uses for this industrial waste product, and that is why you will see soy lecithin in just about everything from food to cosmetics.

Another industrial waste product that ended up in our food supply is fluoride. Hydrofluorosilicic acid is the industrial waste product from the manufacturing of phosphate fertilizers and aluminum and is considered hazardous. It is barreled up and sold across America to communities who add it to their water supply to "prevent tooth decay." Before it was put into our water supply, it was blown out of smokestacks and dumped in rivers, resulting in dead fish and deformed cows. But claiming a health advantage (fewer cavities) gave manufacturers a way to make money "dumping" their waste.

Normally, manufacturers have to pay to get rid of industrial waste. They hit the jackpot.

Even if you live in a community that does not fluoridate the water, you may get more fluoride than you need from processed food. Chicken nuggets, tea, soda, cereal, juice, and infant formula are just some of the processed foods made with fluoridated water. Fluoride disrupts thyroid hormones leading to hypothyroidism, a condition that contributes to obesity.

Over the past 100 years, we have turned industrial waste into food and created fake forms of real food. We have fake butter (margarine), fake whipped cream (Cool Whip), fake eggs (Egg Beaters), fake cheese (Velveeta) and fake bread (Wonder Bread). The only thing that's a "wonder" about Wonder Bread is that it's allowed to be called bread. All of these products have been advertised as healthy alternatives to the real thing, even though they all leave out life-giving nutrients. They are cheap, easy to make in mass quantities, and provide a higher profit margin for food manufacturers. Eating is no longer about health and nourishment; it's all about the bottom line.

Can you guess what this food product is?

WATER, CORN SYRUP, HYDROGENATED VEGETABLE OIL (COCONUT AND PALM KERNEL OILS), HIGH FRUCTOSE CORN SYRUP, LESS THAN 2% OF SODIUM CASEINATE (FROM MILK), NATURAL AND ARTIFICIAL FLAVOR, XANTHAN AND GUAR GUMS, POLYSORBATE 60, SORBITAN MONOSTEARATE, BETA CAROTENE (COLOR).

No, it's not transmission fluid, but it is a knock-off of a food containing heavy cream, sugar, and vanilla extract. That's right, it's Cool Whip—a food designed to replace whipped cream, yet it doesn't even contain cream.

How does fake food get promoted over real food?

Fake food vs. real food

Crisco turned out to contain harmful trans fats, but Proctor and Gamble didn't know that when they marketed it as a replacement for lard. Food manufacturers realized that Crisco was cheaper to buy than butter or lard, and it had the added benefit of extending the shelf life of any food made with it. From the food company perspective, Crisco and its cousin margarine were money makers, so no one bothered to consider the health implications. After all, the number one concern of every business is the bottom line, and most companies will do whatever it takes to stay in the black, including carrying out their own "scientific" studies designed to prove the health benefits of their fake foods.

In the 1950s, a theory popped up claiming that saturated fats were unhealthy. This was a godsend for the food industry because it provided a legitimate reason to use Crisco and margarine over lard and butter. Now the food companies could increase their bottom lines under the guise of improving the health of consumers. The food manufacturers latched on to the anti-saturated fat theory and propelled it forward, unaware of the fact that they were actually doing more harm than good.

In the 1960s, trans fats were found to be harmful, but the food industry wasn't willing to let go of the goose that lays the golden eggs. They did everything possible to keep the deadly saturated fat theory alive. Extensive research was carried out on trans fats in the 1970s and 80s, all demonstrating the harmful effects on humans, but it took over twenty years for the FDA to do anything about it, mostly because the food industry lobbyists fought off the attack on trans fat. The FDA, when it could no longer ignore the evidence, finally required the labeling of trans fats in 2006.

Now the food industry has a problem. The goose (trans fat) is ready to fly south for the winter, but the owner can't live without his golden eggs. He has shareholders to appease and mortgages to pay, so he hides the goose as long as he possibly can. When the goose finally gets out, the owner has to come up with a backup plan. He can't go back to the good old-fashioned geese (butter and lard) because he won't get any golden eggs. Somehow, he has to keep the goose and convince people his goose is better than the old-fashioned kind. So he puts a costume on the goose.

Trans fats were found to be bad for our bodies, but we couldn't just go back to butter and lard. The health authorities would look pretty stupid, and the food companies would lose money. Instead of going back to saturated animal fats, they would fully hydrogenate the vegetable oils rather than partially hydrogenating them. This would decrease the amount of trans fats, providing a false sense of security for the customer but enabling food manufacturers to continue using cheap oils. Problem solved. Keep bashing animal fats and praise fully hydrogenated fats. Of course, fully hydrogenating a fat turns it into a "bad" saturated fat, but no one needs to know that. Another disguise for trans fat is interesterified fats: different chemistry, but same vegetable oils.

That is how misinformation and fake food get going. Someone has a product they need to sell, so they find a way to sell it, usually by coming up with some health claim or false allegation. That someone holds on tight to everything that increases the sale of that product and tries to bury anything that would decrease the sale of that product. Companies conduct studies in-house to prove their fake products are healthier than real food. The focus is on the money. With our capitalist system, we have publicly-traded companies that do everything possible to bring in a profit for their shareholders. Unfortunately, making a substantial profit and creating healthy foods don't always mix, and the consumer suffers the consequences of poor health, unaware that the nutrition information they are fed is not scientifically sound and not in their best interests.

Misinformation spreads

Splenda, an artificial sweetener, is another example of the use of false claims to promote a product. The makers of Splenda claimed that it was made from real sugar when it is actually a synthetic product made from dextrose, maltodextrin, 4-chloro-4-deoxyalpha, D-Galactopyranosyl-1, 6-dichloro-1, dideoxy-beta and D-fructofuranoside. The makers of Equal, another artificial sweetener and Splenda's competition, took them to court and forced Splenda to stop using the false claim "made from real sugar." But the damage had already been done. Most Americans still believe that Splenda is made from real sugar.

Food manufacturers are not the only source of misinformation. The Food Guide Pyramid, sponsored by the USDA, is touted as the healthiest diet on the planet. School cafeterias and food labels are smothered with pictures of the food pyramid with information on how to use it. The pyramid is the foundation for all the nutritional programs in schools, universities, and supermarkets. Even the Boy and Girl Scouts of America teach the Food Guide Pyramid.

The Pyramid recommends a diet high in carbohydrates with breads and cereals at the base of the pyramid (the largest section) and fats at the tip. The USDA is in the business of promoting agricultural products like grains and legumes, so it is very interesting to see those foods at or near the base of the pyramid. Currently, no studies exist to demonstrate the healthiness of the Food Guide Pyramid. We are told it is healthy by the USDA and indoctrinated into that belief in early childhood, in spite of the fact that there is absolutely no evidence to support that view. The Food Guide Pyramid was specifically designed to boost the sale of agricultural products. It was not designed to promote health and wellbeing.

Who benefits financially from the use of fake foods and the low-fat, food guide pyramid diet? The food industry, pharmaceutical industry, health industry, diet industry, and anti-aging industry.

Locally grown, fresh food cannot be mass produced and nationally distributed as it would spoil on the journey from California to New York, so purveyors of real food remain the "little guy." On the other hand, mass industrial food processing is designed to have large distribution channels that generate large sums of money, making industrial food the "big guy." A large corporation that markets a product such as margarine (artificial butter) can make claims that it is healthier than butter, even though the product actually destroys the health of consumers, because it has a lot of disposable income to pay for TV commercials and magazine ads. The "little guy" doesn't have the funds or the resources to counteract the attack on real food, so the truth doesn't get out. The "big guy" has lawyers and lobbyists in key locations to fend off government agencies, such as the FDA, that should be protecting citizens from dangerous foods rather than allowing false health claims for them.

The butter/margarine wars are an excellent example of how this plays out. Next time you cruise down the butter aisle at your local supermarket, take a look at the names given to margarine products—Smart Balance, Smart Choice, and Smart Beat are just a few of the brands you'll find. The manufacturers of these spreads imply by the above names that real butter should be called Dumb Butter, Moron Fat, or Stupid Spread. Their very names imply that butter is for stupid, uneducated people, and any enlightened, well-educated, health-conscious person would choose margarine.

Butter has been one of the healthiest foods in the world, nourishing millions of people for thousands of years. Real butter can't be manufactured in a laboratory, which means that it is more expensive and less able to travel. Margarine manufacturers are able to use cheap oils to create the fake butter in a laboratory. Because the ingredients are cheaper, margarine manufacturers have higher profit margins. They use some of this extra money in ad campaigns designed to convince consumers that margarine is better than butter.

Food companies get to use cheaper ingredients so they can increase their bottom line. These cheap ingredients do not nourish the body, so people get sick. Money is poured into the healthcare system (doctors, hospitals, etc.) to treat these sick people. Pharmaceutical companies make a fortune on drugs designed to treat, but not cure, these diseases, and most of these drugs have side effects that require additional drugs to combat the other drugs. People get tired of being fat and sick, so they go on a diet. But the diet industry tells people to eat fake food and follow the food guide pyramid, creating more marketing opportunities for diet plans, pills, and potions that don't work, starting the vicious cycle all over again.

Turning industrial waste into food and creating imitations of real food expanded P&G's bottom line financially, but it also expanded the bottoms and waists of their customers. Not to worry, the diet industry is standing by with the latest breakthrough, pill, or surgery, ready to "fix" the problem for a few months. When that doesn't work, the pharmaceutical industry is ready with their bag of drugs; of course, you'll have to go see your doctor to get a prescription. The more closely we follow the low-fat, food-guide-pyramid diet, the more closely we begin to resemble the food pyramid—not much on top but bigger and bigger on the bottom!

The problem with fake food

Before the advent of fake food, people cooked from scratch with ingredients that were easy to pronounce. Families ate meals together and chronic diseases were practically unknown. Fake food has changed all that. Instead of eating foods grown on the land, we eat foods manufactured in a laboratory from synthetic ingredients. Families lose bonding opportunities when they replace a home-cooked family dinner with individual TV dinners or fast food while Junior runs off to band practice and Mom heads to the PTA meeting. Fake food has made it possible for people to live together without knowing each other. We are able to maintain our hectic lifestyles of running from one event to another because we can grab something from a box or can that can be fixed in a jiffy.

The rise of fake food has paralleled the rise of heart disease, diabetes, cancer, ADHD, autism, and obesity. If you really want to lose weight and get healthy, it's time to get back in the kitchen with real food. Traditional cultures knew what was healthy to eat and passed that knowledge on from generation to generation because they loved their children and wanted the best for them. Today, we get our information from commercials, advertisements, and marketing gurus whose first priority is the health of their business, not the health of us or our children.

We are in a situation where the government and health authorities are warning us about the dangers of real food (i.e., the saturated fat in butter) while doctors are on TV encouraging the use of fake food (margarine). How can all the media, government officials, doctors and healthcare professionals be wrong? How could any thinking American not believe these authorities are telling the truth?

One of the greatest challenges we face as consumers is trying to do what's best for ourselves and our families while swimming in a sea of deception and misinformation. We invite you to join us on the journey to freedom as we liberate you from the confusion and give you every thing you need to stay fit and healthy.

TAKE HOME MESSAGE

1. Eat real food the way God made it.

2. Do not follow the food guide pyramid or the low-fat diet.

3. Don't believe everything the health authorities tell you.

HOW MEDICINE BECAME DRUG DRIVEN

Before 1910, there were no standards for doctors to follow. While there were some good medical schools in existence, many doctors were able to pay a small fee for a mail-order medical degree. Clearly, this was not in the best interests of the public, and the American Medical Association attempted some in-house cleaning. The feeble attempt failed because committee members could not agree on a set of standards for physicians, and they also did not have the funding necessary to tackle this gigantic problem.

In the early 1900s, Andrew Carnegie and John D. Rockefeller developed an interest in pharmaceuticals. Rockefeller established the Institute for Medical Research in 1901, and Simon Flexner was on the board of directors. Simon's brother, Abraham Flexner, was on staff at the Carnegie Foundation for the Advancement of Teaching.

In December 1908, Henry S. Pritchett, president of the Carnegie Foundation, and Abraham Flexner met with the AMA and discussed the problems with medicine and physician standards. The AMA agreed to let the Carnegie Foundation take over their efforts to improve the medical field.

The Flexner Report, published in 1910 by Abraham Flexner with the help of his brother Simon, pointed out the problems in medicine and provided some sound solutions against which no one could argue. Some kind of reform was definitely needed to protect citizens from uneducated physicians. But the report suggested putting more emphasis on pharmacology and also recommended adding research departments to qualified schools.

With an interest in pharmaceuticals and billions of dollars at their disposal, Carnegie and Rockefeller gained control of medical schools and the training of physicians. In 1908, 160 medical schools were in existence, many of them teaching nutrition and natural therapies, but that number decreased to only 80 schools by 1927.

Carnegie and Rockefeller set up an accreditation for medical schools. Any school that agreed to teach about drugs instead of nutrition was accredited. Only accredited schools received funding and research departments. Naturally, homeopathic schools and other institutions wanting to teach nutrition went bankrupt and were forced out of business.

Today, medical students spend most of their time learning about drugs and little time learning about nutrition. There is so much information packed into their training that they don't have time for independent thinking. That is why Western medicine is so heavy into the use of pharmaceuticals. It has nothing to do with health or science, but everything to do with money.

Lipid Profiling

Start with one proud researcher and two seriously flawed studies. Add a dash of politics, a few food industry gurus, and a reporter with no nutrition knowledge, and what do you have? A controversial low-fat diet turned into dogma.

Have you ever wondered why our beliefs about fat and cholesterol keep changing? Beginning in the 1960s, Americans were encouraged to use margarine instead of butter. Then in 2005, headlines warned of the health dangers of trans fats, which are found in margarine, **but health organizations today still recommend margarine over butter.** Eggs were bad for us between the mid 1980s and late 1990s, but now they are good for us. Polyunsaturated vegetable oils such as soybean and corn were given the green light until it was determined that they cause cancer and then monounsaturated fats found in olive oil took the spotlight. Today polyunsaturated fats (soybean oil) and monounsaturated fats (olive oil) share the limelight and the cancer issues have been swept under the rug.

How is the average consumer, like you, supposed to know what is true and what isn't when the "truth" keeps changing? To clear the confusion, we need to go back to the beginning of the fat and cholesterol story, starting with the proud researcher.

The fat theory

It all started in the 1950s with the development of the technology to measure blood cholesterol levels. This enabled researcher Ancel Keys to formulate his famous hypothesis that saturated fat and cholesterol in the diet caused heart disease. Real scientists will come up with a hypothesis, or theory, and try to prove the hypothesis wrong. If they can't disprove the hypothesis, then it is considered a good theory and becomes known as fact. The reason real scientists try to disprove their theory is that it helps them stay objective and they are less likely to ignore evidence that disagrees with their theory. Ancel Keys was not a real scientist. He was more in love with his theory than with the scientific evidence, and instead of trying to disprove his hypothesis, he set out to prove it.

Key's theory is based on two studies. The first reported by David Kritchevsky involved rabbits. Kritchevsky fed pure cholesterol to rabbits and noticed that they developed a form of plaque in their arteries, similar to but not quite the same as the plaque found in human arteries. The second study, called the "seven countries study," was carried out by Keys himself. Keys was able to show on a graph that the more fat available for consumption in a country (note this is not the amount of fat actually consumed by people) correlated positively with the death rate from heart disease in that country. These studies sound convincing. But are they?

Rabbits are herbivores (plant eaters) and cholesterol is found only in animal foods, so rabbits are unable to process cholesterol. The only place for the cholesterol to go is in the tissues. That is why Kritchevsky found cholesterol in the arteries. He also found cholesterol plaque in the organs of the rabbits, which we do not find in humans, but Keys conveniently ignored this fact. Since rabbits and humans have totally different physiologies, we cannot extrapolate from a rabbit to a human, so these rabbit studies are completely useless in the fat/cholesterol argument.

The seven countries study is interesting in that at the time of the study, data was available for twenty-two countries. If you put all twenty-two countries on Keys's graph, you will find no correlation between fat availability and heart disease death. It appears that Keys handpicked the countries that would prove his theory and ignored the other fifteen countries that disproved his theory. That is not good science. If we all carried out experiments like that, we could prove or disprove anything we wanted.

Despite their many flaws and unscientific nature, these two studies form the foundation of our views on fat and cholesterol. But the story doesn't end there.

Fat phobia

In 1961, the American Heart Association (AHA) introduced the prudent diet, which called for margarine and vegetable oil instead of butter, cold cereal instead of eggs and chicken and fish instead of red meat. Keys was on the board that approved this diet even though he found out in 1958 that trans fats were unhealthy and he knew margarine was a source of trans fat.

Surprisingly, there exists a study comparing the prudent diet (high in vegetable oil) to a diet high in animal foods that was published in the *Journal of the American Medical Association* in 1966. The study, called the Anti-Coronary Club, began in 1957 and compared two groups of New York businessmen aged 40 to 59 years. One group followed the prudent diet and the other group ate eggs for breakfast and meat three times a day.

The average serum cholesterol level of the prudent group was 220 mg/dl compared to 250mg/dl in the egg-and-meat-eating group. Can you guess which group had the most deaths from heart disease? If you picked the egg-and-meat-eating group, you'd be wrong. Even though the men in the prudent group had lower cholesterol levels, eight of them died from heart disease while absolutely no deaths occurred in the egg-and-meat group.

Had Keys been a real scientist, he would have tossed out his theory after this study or at least questioned its validity. But, he ignored it along with everyone else. The study did not get media attention because it disagreed with the theory that animal fat and cholesterol were unhealthy.

Now we come to the politics. Senator George McGovern got on the nutritional platform in 1968 by forming McGovern's Committee on Nutrition and Human Needs. The original purpose was to address the problems of malnutrition, but by the mid 1970s, the emphasis changed to over-nutrition. In 1976, McGovern commissioned labor reporter Nick Motten to write the Dietary Goals for the United States. Motten had no training or experience with nutrition or health so he relied solely on information provided to him by Mark Hegsted, a Harvard School of Public Health nutritionist. Hegsted recommended a low-fat diet even though he admitted his opinion was rather extreme, and he has since changed his view on fat.

The first Dietary Goals recommending a low-fat, low-saturated-fat diet came out in 1977 but they did not receive unanimous support. The American Medical Association, scientist E. H. "Pete" Ahrens, Robert Levy, director of the National Heart Lung and Blood Institute (NHLBI), and others did not support the low-fat recommendations. Ahrens was an expert on lipid metabolism and the man behind the *Journal of Lipid Research*. The dairy council, cattle herders, and egg board did not agree with the recommendations, either, for obvious reasons.

McGovern's committee began to fizzle out, so the United States Department of Agriculture (USDA) picked up the dietary goals. The USDA was in the business of promoting agricultural products such as grains, corn and beans—all carbohydrate-rich foods. They liked the idea of a low-fat diet because if people cut the fat from their diets, they would have to add carbohydrates.

While the USDA was trying to convince the public to eat less total fat and animal fat, the National Academy of Sciences published their pamphlet *Towards Healthful Diets*, encouraging Americans to watch their weight rather than worry about the fat content of their diet.

Several studies were carried out between the 1960s and 1980s to demonstrate the harmful effects of animal fat and cholesterol, but none of them offered any proof for the theory.

One study was published in 1965 in the *British Medical Journal*. Researchers divided patients who had already had a heart attack into three groups. One group received polyunsaturated corn oil, another group received monounsaturated olive oil and the third group received saturated animal fats. Two years later the corn oil group had lowered their cholesterol by 30% but only 52% of the subjects remained alive. About 57% of the olive oil group remained alive at the end of two years, whereas 75% of the animal fat group remained alive. This study never received media attention because it did not support Keys's hypothesis. Most doctors and dietitians don't even know it exists.

The NIH conducted studies in Honolulu, Puerto Rico, Chicago, and Framingham (Massachusetts), but could not find any evidence to support a low-fat diet. In 1992, Framingham director William Castelli even said in the *Archives of Internal Medicine*, "In Framingham, Mass., the more saturated fat one ate, the more cholesterol one ate, the more calories one ate, the lower the people's serum cholesterol. ... We found that the people who ate the most cholesterol, ate the most saturated fat, ate the most calories, weighed the least and were the most physically active." Not good news for the low-fat bandwagon.

The Multiple Risk Factor Intervention Trial sponsored by the NHLBI was one of the major studies in the 1980s and involved over 12,000 men. The subjects were divided into two groups. Both groups were told to stop smoking and lower fat intake, and high blood pressure was brought under control. One group received more care and instruction in preventing heart disease while the other group received the usual care. At the end of the study, 17.9 people per 1,000 died from heart disease in the stepped-up care group compared to 19.3 people per 1,000 in the usual care group, but there were more deaths from all causes in the stepped-up care group than the usual care group. Since multiple risk factors were dealt with in this study, we cannot conclude that lowering saturated fat prevented death from heart disease. It may have been the stabilized blood pressure or the lack of smoking that accounted for the small difference in death rate.

The Lipid Research Clinic Coronary Primary Prevention Trial (LRCCPPT) is the most popular study used to prove that saturated fat and cholesterol are bad. This study had two groups. Both groups were put on a low-fat, low-cholesterol diet and received diet instructions from a registered dietitian, but one group received a cholesterol-lowering drug as well. Fewer people died from heart disease in the drug group, but more people in the drug group died from cancer, stroke, suicide, and violence. Independent researchers could find no statistically significant reduction in heart disease death between the two groups. The problem with this study is that it didn't actually test a low-fat, low-cholesterol diet since both groups were on the same diet. It only tested a cholesterol-lowering drug, so we cannot conclude from this study that a low-fat/cholesterol diet prevents heart disease. Also, the study only involved middle-aged men who had cholesterol levels higher than ninety-five percent of the population, so we can't use this study to make any kind of recommendations for women, young adults, the elderly, or children. But the media took hold of this study and spread the message that saturated fat and cholesterol were killers. One of the problems with non-scientists reporting on scientific research is that they don't have a clue how to interpret research data.

If the research couldn't come up with conclusive evidence to support a low fat diet, why are we so afraid of fat?

By the mid 1980s it was clear that fat was a controversial subject, so the NIH decided to hold a "Consensus Conference" to clear up the confusion and tell anxious Americans what to eat. They were also hoping to justify the use of taxpayer money to fund worthless studies. The conference leaders happened to be major players in the LRCCPPT study. The theory behind the conference was that scientists would come together, discuss the issue for two days and agree on a finding, namely that saturated fat and cholesterol were villains. Several prominent people in the scientific and medical communities spoke out against a low-fat diet, but the final report made no mention of the dissenters. According to the report, everyone agreed that fat and cholesterol were bad.

The AMA still wasn't on board with the anti-fat agenda, so the NIH, which receives a lot of funding from the pharmaceutical industry, launched the National Cholesterol Education Program (NCEP) to educate physicians about the dangers of saturated fat and cholesterol. The program worked. The AMA finally came on board.

To sum up, one guy comes up with a theory and concocts a study to support his view. Then politicians, food lobbyists, and a clueless reporter sign on to write dietary guidelines for Americans. Next, they conduct studies to prove to the public that their guidelines are sound, but the studies actually prove the opposite so they are either ignored or misinterpreted. And finally the pharmaceutical-backed NIH launches a huge campaign to convince doctors to agree to the controversial guidelines. Enter the media, which takes this controversial and unscientific belief and turns it into dogma.

Ever wonder why we call the French a paradox? They eat a lot of saturated fat yet they have much less heart disease than Americans. The unfortunate truth is that Americans have been indoctrinated into the low-fat cult, so instead of changing our views to match science, we ignore or label the truth as something else. Some will say the reduced rate of heart disease in the French is due to wine consumption. If that's true, then why don't we do what the French do? Eat lots of saturated fat with red wine. It clearly works better than our low-fat diet, and it tastes better, too.

Low fat and low cholesterol are not working! That is why the government and pharmaceutical companies keep doing studies on low-fat/cholesterol diets. **After fifty years of research, they are still trying to find proof for their theory!** Why? Because the food and pharmaceutical industries make a lot of money selling fake food and medication. Food companies can add inexpensive corn syrup to peanut butter, take out some fat, slap on a health claim and sell it at a higher price, all because it has less fat than the regular product. Lipitor, a cholesterol-lowering drug, is expensive and the number one selling prescription drug in America. You can bet the food and pharmaceutical industries won't let the fat/cholesterol theory die without a fight.

While the food and pharmaceutical industries pad their pockets with low fat dogma, consumers suffer the side effects. Our focus on cholesterol as the cause of heart disease has blinded us to the real culprits behind heart disease, such as mineral deficiencies, inflammation, and infections. We suffer unnecessary stress worrying about our cholesterol levels and eat a fabricated diet devoid of nutrition to lower cholesterol. Both stress and lack of nutrients can lead to heart disease.

The truth about fat

Most healthcare providers still believe saturated fat and cholesterol cause heart disease because that is what they are taught to believe in school. Few bother to look up the evidence for themselves, so they still promote vegetable oils over animal fats.

Vegetable oils are mostly polyunsaturated fats that have more than one double bond. The more double bonds in a fat, the more unstable the fat. Unstable fats go rancid quickly and are a major cause of inflammation that can damage arterial walls and cells in the body. The processing of vegetable oils is harsh, and by the time these oils find their way to supermarket shelves, they are already rancid. These rancid oils are then heated to high temperatures in cooking or baking, causing further damage.

The American public is completely unaware of the dangers of soybean, corn, cottonseed, and canola oils. Even in their liquid form, they increase the need for vitamin E and other antioxidants, and they disrupt prostaglandin formation leading to an increased tendency for heart attack. Most vegetable oils today are consumed in the form of hydrogenated fats, or trans fat. Hydrogen molecules are added to liquid vegetable oils to create a fat that is more solid at room temperature and more useful in baked goods, but the chemical structure of the fat is changed into something that does not exist in nature. Following are just some of the adverse effects of trans fats on the human body:

- Alters enzymes that neutralize carcinogens.
- Interferes with the body's use of omega-3 fats.
- Increases blood insulin levels leading to Type II diabetes.
- Decreases testosterone (low testosterone is a risk factor for heart disease in men).

- Causes blood platelet stickiness.

- Increases lipoprotein-a (a risk factor for heart disease) and LDL, and decreases HDL.

- Causes infertility and breastfeeding problems.

In the late 1980s, the low fat/saturated fat cause was taken up by the largely vegetarian organization, Center for Science in the Public Interest (CSPI). CSPI mounted their white horse proclaiming the dangers of animal fats, coconut, and palm oils all in the guise of protecting consumers. Vegetarians, of course, do not want people eating animal fats. Through heavy campaigns, they managed to convince fast food chains and food manufacturers to use hydrogenated oils full of unhealthy trans fat, instead of saturated lard and beef tallow. Of interest is the fact that the replacement of animal fats with trans fats corresponds to the skyrocketing rates of obesity between 1980 and 2000.

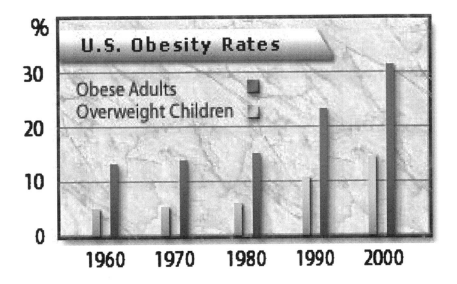

We don't think it was in the public's best interest to switch from natural animal fats to fabricated trans fats.

Trans fats are finally getting the bad rap they deserve, but food manufacturers don't want to give up the cheap vegetable oils, so they are changing the nature of vegetable oils with a new process called interesterification. Interesterification involves completely hydrogenating a vegetable oil and then chemically rearranging the fatty acids to provide a more stable fat. But interesterification may be even worse than trans fat because it interferes with fat and glucose metabolism leading to insulin-dependent diabetes.

As we have decreased saturated fat and increased vegetable oils in the diet, we have seen huge increases in heart disease, cancer, diabetes, and obesity. So, instead of relying on man to come up with a healthy fat that tastes good, we need to go back to the fats God created. After all, He knew what He was doing. Animal fats are in fact very healthy, and most of the health problems and diseases we've experienced over the past forty years are in part due to the lack of saturated fat in the diet.

Saturated fats, due to their more solid and stable structure, give cells their shape and prevent premature wrinkling. Vegetable oils, because they are liquid and very unstable, cannot give much structure to cells. When we eat a lot of vegetable fats, we begin to resemble prunes because our cells can't hold their shape. This has spawned the anti-aging industry, which manufactures all sorts of creams and lotions from a variety of chemicals that help smooth out the wrinkles.

The brain is about fifty percent saturated fat, and all the organs in your body are surrounded by saturated fat, especially the heart. The heart uses the saturated fat surrounding it for energy because we could not physically eat enough in a day to meet the energy demands of the heart. **The heart gets its fuel from saturated fat, and it is the only organ in the body that does not succumb to cancer.** Other benefits of saturated fat include:

- Makes up one-hundred percent of lung surfactant (the protective lining in the lung).
- Protects liver from alcohol and toxins (medications).
- Component of cellular membranes.
- Signaling and stabilization processes.

- Hormone production.
- Boosts immune function.
- Promotes healthy kidneys.
- Puts calcium into bones.
- Decreases lipoprotein a (a marker for heart disease).

Cholesterol is also critically important to good health. Without cholesterol, we would die, and that is why the body makes most of the cholesterol we need. Studies have shown that people with higher cholesterol levels actually live longer. Cholesterol functions as an antioxidant and naturally increases as we age. We tend to accumulate more free radicals as we age, requiring more antioxidants to get rid of them. Other functions of cholesterol include:

- Vitamin D synthesis.
- Building block for hormones.
- Component of cell membranes.
- Involved in memory and cognition.
- Component of scar tissue.
- Aids in digestion of fats.

The more cholesterol we eat, the less the body makes; the less we eat, the more the body makes. When we see high cholesterol levels (over 350 mg/dl) we should be asking what is going on in the body that requires extra antioxidants. High cholesterol is a sign of something else failing to work properly in the body, not a disease that needs to be treated.

Cholesterol can do damage if it is oxidized, and the most effective way to oxidize cholesterol is to follow the food-guide-pyramid, vegetable-oil diet recommended by most doctors and dietitians.

The truth about saturated fat and cholesterol is finally coming out. It is time to put these healthy nutrients back in the diet.

TAKE HOME MESSAGE

1. Saturated fat and cholesterol do not cause heart disease.

2. Eat butter, lard, beef tallow, coconut oil, and palm oil.

3. Eat high-cholesterol foods such as eggs and organ meats.

4. Eat full-fat dairy foods.

5. Avoid hydrogenated or interesterified fats.

6. Avoid soybean, corn, cottonseed, and canola oils

The Carbohydrate Craze

Weird is not too strong a word to describe the evolution of the high carbohydrate diet, as it has more to do with sex than science. Believe it or not, carbohydrate foods were foisted on the American public to prevent sexual sins and excesses, and this is the origin of the term "moral fiber."

Screwy logic

The raunchy tale begins in the 1800s when the Reverend Sylvester Graham developed an interest in health, focusing on vegetarianism, abstinence from alcohol, and the prevention of sexual desires and lusts. He believed that eating meat caused one to become sexually excited, and he cited masturbation as the cause of most health problems. Graham went around lecturing on the evils of sex, causing quite an uproar, so he eventually gave up the lectures and focused on nutrition. After all, the proper diet could control carnal passions. His "cure" included exercise, sex only once a month for married couples, and a vegetarian diet that included the Graham cracker, a coarse flat bread made with whole wheat flour. The cracker was used to promote more frequent bowel movements as supposedly fecal matter in the colon put too much pressure on the genitals, creating unhealthy desires.

Graham influenced James Caleb Jackson, who combined Graham's diet with hydrotherapy (extremely cold showers and wet packs). Jackson invented Granula, a wafer made from graham flour and water, that he fed to patients at his sanitarium in New York. Ellen G. White, founder of the Seventh Day Adventists, visited this sanitarium on the advice of an angel and eventually set up her own sanitarium in Battle Creek, Michigan. The sanitarium floundered until Dr. John Harvey Kellogg took over operations.

Kellogg was a vegetarian and also believed that sexual desires were the cause of most ailments. He was so extreme in his view on sex that his marriage to Ella Eaton was never consummated, and they had separate sleeping quarters their entire marriage. They adopted all of their children.

A disciple of Graham, Kellogg was always experimenting with whole grains. He invented a biscuit made from oatmeal and cornmeal and called it Granula, copying Jackson's invention. Kellogg renamed the product Granola after losing the resulting lawsuit. He fed the sanitarium patients a vegetarian diet with meat substitutes and his whole grain concoctions. Since none of the patients were really ill to begin with, they all made remarkable recoveries. Most of the patients were admitted for rest and relaxation.

Influenced by Henry Perky's Shredded Wheat, Kellogg created the first flaked cereal called Granose, which started a cereal and health food revolution in Battle Creek. C.W. Post, also a cereal inventor, spent time as a patient in Kellogg's sanitarium. He was fascinated with the diet and went on to invent Grape Nuts and Postum, a cereal-based coffee alternative. Post used health claims and made up diseases to promote all his products. Postum "made red blood cells" and prevented the disease "coffee neuralgia," while Grape Nuts would "cure consumption, malaria, and loose teeth." (We assume the loose teeth just fell out while crunching on the hard cereal.) He didn't provide any evidence for these health claims, he just said what he wanted to say to convince people to buy his products. It worked, and other food manufacturers began to copy his technique; invent a health claim, sell a product.

Eventually, the Kellogg Cereal Company was formed at the hand of John Harvey's brother, W.K. Kellogg. John Harvey Kellogg lived long enough to see his ideas about sex refuted by the medical establishment, but he was the kind of person who was never wrong. There you have the beginning of the high carbohydrate diet. No science, just misinformation and nonsense.

The truth about carbohydrates

Carbohydrates are no longer attached to sex, but they are still foisted on unsuspecting Americans with unscientific claims. Foods high in carbohydrates include breads, cereals, pasta, dried beans and peas, starchy vegetables and fruits. All these foods are at the base of the Food Guide Pyramid, but are they really good for us?

There are essential fats and proteins, but no essential carbohydrates. The body can make all the carbohydrate it needs, so we do not need a dietary source to survive. Yet the health police recommend that at least fifty percent of total calories in the diet come from carbohydrates. Why do we need so much of something that the body doesn't require?

We don't, but the food and agricultural industries make money on carbohydrates so they want us to be eating more of them. When the four basic food groups came out, equal amounts of foods from dairy, protein, grains, and fruits and vegetables were recommended. That all changed with the Food Guide Pyramid, when grains became the emphasis of the diet. Grains were put on the bottom of the pyramid, and Americans were encouraged to get six to eleven grain servings a day. This change was not based on science, but on the USDA's need to increase the sale of agricultural products.

Sugar and fiber are the two components of carbohydrates that wreak havoc on the body. All carbohydrate foods are broken down into sugar (glucose) in the body. Carbohydrates, and to some extent protein, are the only nutrients in the diet that raise blood sugar levels. When we eat a high-carbohydrate meal, the body quickly converts those carbs into glucose and sends the glucose into the blood stream. The blood stream can only handle so much glucose before it causes coma or death, so the body has to clear this sugar out. The hormone insulin is secreted from the pancreas to unlock cell doors so glucose can enter the cells to provide energy. Once the cells are amply supplied, insulin tells the liver to send the remaining glucose into glycogen and fat storage.

The first problem with a high-carbohydrate diet is that it encourages the body to store fat. While in fat-storage mode, the body can't take fat from storage to use as energy, which makes losing weight a bit difficult. Carbohydrates basically mess up fat metabolism by stimulating the secretion of insulin. Insulin is the only hormone that puts fat into storage. All the other hormones, such as those from the adrenal and thyroid glands, take fat out of storage.

As we repeatedly assault our bodies with carbohydrates, insulin becomes the dominant hormone and controls every other hormone. Insulin is an anabolic hormone along with testosterone, estrogen, progesterone, and growth hormone. They are anabolic because they build up the body (store fat, grow bone, etc.). Glucagon, which works opposite to insulin and releases fat from storage, is a catabolic hormone, along with hormones from the thyroid and adrenal glands. They are catabolic because they tear down the body (take fat out of storage, etc.). The body wants to be in balance between building up and tearing down.

If insulin levels are high, as they are when on a high carbohydrate diet, the body has to compensate. One way to compensate is to decrease the other anabolic hormones. A decrease in growth hormone can stunt growth in children and cause fat accumulation in adults as well as a lowered sex drive (the pharmaceutical industry invented the drug Viagra for carbohydrate lovers to combat a low sex drive). A decrease in sex hormones can cause problems with fertility and, in men, heart disease. Another option is to increase the catabolic hormones. This leads to problems such as a weakened immune system and hyperthyroidism. Higher levels of catabolic hormones means more breakdown of body tissues, which can lead to damaged arterial walls and, therefore, heart disease. Either way, compensating for excessive insulin levels harms the body and decreases quality of life.

Most carbohydrate foods are composed of different combinations of glucose, fructose, and galactose, with glucose being the most common. Table sugar and high fructose corn syrup are a combination of glucose and fructose, whereas potatoes contain long chains of glucose. Lactose, the sugar in milk, is a combination of glucose and galactose. When we eat carbohydrates, they are broken down into these simple sugars. The simple sugars are sent to the liver, but most of the glucose escapes into the bloodstream.

The liver converts fructose into fat more than any other sugar. The more fructose you eat, the more likely you are to store fat. Excessive fructose can also cause fatty liver and cirrhosis, just like excessive alcohol. Americans are eating a lot of fructose from the three to five servings of fruits we are supposed to have daily, the high fructose corn syrup that is in just about everything, and the new natural sweetener, agave nectar, which is ninety percent fructose.

For years, diabetics were taught to use fructose instead of table sugar because fructose doesn't raise blood sugar as quickly as glucose. In other words, fructose has a lower glycemic index (GI) than glucose. The rage these days is to consume carbs that are low on the glycemic index—carbs that don't spike your blood sugar. Most people assume that low glycemic is a synonym for complex or whole grain and high glycemic means refined, but this is not the case at all. Soda, a sugary beverage that has absolutely no nutritional value, is a low-glycemic food, while millet, a type of whole grain loaded with vitamins and minerals, is a high-glycemic food. Many candies are also low on the glycemic index, so it's possible to eat a low GI diet that provides inadequate amounts of vitamins, minerals, and antioxidants.

The glycemic index of a food can be manipulated by other foods. For example, putting butter and sour cream on a baked potato lowers the glycemic index of the potato. Eating a salad containing oil and vinegar dressing will lower the glycemic index of the meal. Fat, protein, and acid all slow down the release of sugar into the blood stream. Because a low GI diet is not always a healthy diet due to the effect of other foods on carbohydrates, it is a waste of time to determine the GI of a food before eating it. The Liberation Diet presented in this book is a naturally low-GI diet that provides the vitamins, minerals, and antioxidants needed by the body to keep you healthy.

The second problem with a high carbohydrate diet is that it results in high blood sugar levels. Sugar reacts with protein and fat. If you have a lot of sugar in the blood, it will collide with protein molecules and cell membranes (fats), destroying the ability of these proteins and fats to function. These reactions are called glycation reactions. The more sugar you have in the blood, the faster and more frequent these destructive reactions occur. These glycation products can damage the lens of the eye, collagen, tendons, and the myelin sheath surrounding nerves, leading to vision problems, arthritis, and other inflammatory diseases. Damaged cell membranes can also make the cells vulnerable to cancer cells.

A high blood sugar level means a high insulin level, and excess insulin causes a rise in the hormone gastrin. Gastrin produces acid in the stomach, which is necessary for digestion, but too much gastrin means too much acid. The results are gastritis, ulcers, and reflux disease.

While the sugar component of carbohydrates causes obesity and stomach problems, the fiber component of carbohydrates weakens the digestive tract. Every day, teachers, doctors, and commercials tout the benefits of fiber. Some studies suggest that high-fiber breakfast cereals aid weight loss, and other studies claim fiber prevents colon cancer. The fiber recommendation is now up to thirty-five grams a day; that's over four cups of All-Bran daily! But is fiber all it's cracked up to be?

Keep in mind that, in research studies, high-fiber diets are compared to high-sugar diets. If you're choice is between high fiber and high sugar, the high fiber is definitely the better option because it won't spike your blood sugar as much as the high sugar. Foods containing fiber also contain more vitamins and minerals than refined and sugary foods. But if you have a choice between high fiber and high fat, you're definitely better off with the high fat, assuming the fats are mostly saturated and monounsaturated with some omega-3 fats.

Fiber blocks the absorption of minerals whereas fats increase the absorption of minerals, vitamins, and antioxidants. Extra water is needed to process fiber, which can dilute nutrients and flush them out of the body before they can be absorbed, but water is created from the processing of fats. Fats actually hydrate the body from the inside out and they don't irritate the lining of the intestines like fiber.

Cows have three "stomachs" to process all the fiber they eat, and their digestive tracts contain bacteria that can digest fiber. Humans have one stomach and do not have the enzymes or bacteria to break down fiber. Why on earth would it be good to eat huge quantities of something we are not designed to digest? Fiber gained its reputation because of its perceived value in preventing sexual sins, not because it provided health and vitality to the body. Vegetarianism and the fear of fat also drives fiber consumption, but with our increasing intake of fiber comes increasing numbers of irritable bowel syndrome, Crohn's disease, ulcerative colitis, diverticular disease, and more. Curiously, the "cure" for these diseases is a low-fiber diet. Hmm—makes one wonder if we shouldn't just start out on a low-fiber diet and prevent these diseases.

Nathan Pritikin thought a very high-carbohydrate, extremely low-fat diet was best for the body. Annette visited the Pritikin Longevity Center in California while in school and had the opportunity to interview some of the residents. The number one complaint was flatulence. Now, passing gas is a normal part of life and we all do it, whether we admit it or not, but these people on the Pritikin diet suffered from excessive flatulence. It was so embarrassing that it nearly snuffed out their social life. Bacteria in the intestines ferment the carbohydrates we eat. More carbs equals increased fermentation in the intestines, which leads to excessive flatulence and bloating.

Fiber expands when wet. When we eat carbohydrate foods, they expand in our stomachs and intestines. This expansion sometimes makes us feel full, but it also stretches out the stomach, which means that we need more and more food to get that satisfied feeling. Fortunately, the stomach will return to normal size once you reduce your intake of carbohydrate foods.

While the stomach is designed to expand, the intestines are not. Carbohydrates can irritate the lining of the intestines and destroy the muscles in the colon that should be used to eliminate waste. With high carbohydrate diets, we lose the ability to use the muscles that push stool along, and the result is constipation. The common cure is more fiber and water. This further decreases muscle tone, and we eventually end up dependent on laxatives.

Some fiber is good for the body and feeds the healthy bacteria in our intestines, but thirty-five grams is excessive. You would have to eat a lot of bran products or take a supplement to get that much fiber in the diet. We know refined grains are unhealthy, but eating just the bran apart from the rest of the grain is unhealthy, too. Grains should be eaten whole, and they should be sprouted, soaked, or sour leavened (proper grain preparation will be discussed in the Superfoods chapter). On the Liberation Diet, you will get just the right amount of fiber, and you won't have to eat any cardboard.

Who benefits from a high carbohydrate diet? It certainly isn't you. If you take a good look at processed food, you'll find that the majority of those foods are carbohydrate based. High fructose corn syrup and grains are inexpensive, so the food industry makes lots of money on products containing them. While the food industry puts money in their pocket, you get to suffer the side effects of excess carbohydrate consumption, which generally means taking money out of your pocket and giving it to your favorite doctor and pharmacist.

LETTER ON CORPULENCE

Addressed to the Public

Barry Groves, Ph.D.*

Nearly 140 years ago, one man changed the thinking on diet completely. It all started with a small booklet entitled *Letter on Corpulence Addressed to the Public*, not written by a dietician or a doctor, but by an undertaker named William Banting. It became one of the most famous books on obesity ever written. First published in 1863, it went into many editions and continued to be published long after the author's death. The book was revolutionary, and it should have changed Western medical thinking on diet for weight loss for ever.

William Banting was well-regarded in nineteenth century society. He was a fine carpenter and an undertaker to the rich and famous. But if he had remained only that, his name would probably be remembered today merely as the Duke of Wellington's coffin maker, if indeed it were remembered at all.

None of Banting's family on either parent's side had any tendency to obesity. However, when he was in his thirties, William started to become overweight, and he consulted an eminent surgeon, a kind personal friend, who recommended increased "bodily exertion before any ordinary daily labors began." Banting had a heavy boat and lived near the river, so he took up rowing the boat for two hours a day. All this did for him, however, was to give him a prodigious appetite. He put on weight and was advised to stop. So much for exercise!

He was then advised that he could remedy his obesity by "moderate and light food," but wasn't really told what was intended by this. He says he brought his system into a low, impoverished state without reducing his weight, which caused many obnoxious boils to appear and two rather formidable carbuncles. He went into hospital and was ably operated upon—but also fed into increased obesity.

Banting went into hospital twenty times in as many years for weight reduction. He tried swimming, walking, riding and taking the sea air. He drank "gallons of physic and liquor potassae"; took the spa waters at Leamington, Cheltenham, and Harrogate, and tried low-calorie, starvation diets; he took Turkish baths at a rate of up to three a week for a year; but lost only six pounds in all that time and had less and less energy.

He was assured by one physician, whom he calls "one of the ablest physicians in the land," that putting weight on was perfectly natural; that he, himself, had put on a pound for every year of manhood and he was not surprised by Banting's condition—he just advised "more exercise, vapour baths and shampooing and medicine."

Banting tried every form of slimming treatment the medical profession could devise but it was all in vain. Eventually, discouraged and disillusioned—and still very fat—he gave up. By 1862 at the age of 64, William Banting weighed 202 pounds and he was only 5'5" tall. Although he was of no great weight or size, still Banting said, "I could not stoop to tie my shoes, so to speak, nor to attend to the little offices humanity requires without considerable pain and difficulty, which only the corpulent can understand. I have been compelled to go downstairs slowly backward to save the jar of increased weight on the knee and ankle joints and have been obliged to puff and blow over every slight exertion, particularly that of going upstairs."

Eventually, in August 1862, Banting consulted a noted Fellow of the Royal College of Surgeons: an ear, nose and throat specialist, Dr. William Harvey. It was an historic meeting. Dr. Harvey had recently returned from a symposium in Paris where he had heard Dr. Claude Bernard, a renowned physiologist, talk of a new theory about the part the liver played in the disease of diabetes. Bernard believed that the liver, as well as secreting bile, also secreted a sugar-like substance that it made from elements of the blood passing through it. This started Harvey's thinking about the roles of the various food elements in diabetes, and he began a major course of research into the whole question of the way in which fats, sugars, and starches affected the body.

When Dr. Harvey met Banting, he was interested as much by Banting's obesity as by his deafness, for he recognized that the one was the cause of the other. So Harvey put Banting on a diet. By Christmas, Banting was down to 184 pounds and, by the following August, 156 pounds.

Harvey's advice to him was to give up bread, butter, milk, sugar, beer and potatoes. These, he was told, contained starch and saccharine matter tending to create fat and were to be avoided altogether. When told what he could not eat, Banting thought that he had very little left to live on. His kind friend soon showed him that really there was ample, and Banting was only too happy to give the plan a fair trial. Within a very few days, he says, he derived immense benefit from it. The plan led to an excellent night's rest with six to eight hours' sleep per night.

Fortunately for us today, Banting was quite a remarkable man. It is for this reason alone that we can know today what this miraculous diet was. In May 1863, at his own expense, Banting published the first edition of his now famous *Letter on Corpulence* in which he tells us of Harvey's diet plan (see below).

On this diet Banting lost nearly one pound per week from August 1862 to August 1863. In his own words he said: "I can confidently state that quantity of diet may safely be left to the natural appetite; and that it is quality only which is essential to abate and cure corpulence."

After thirty-eight weeks. Banting felt better than he had for the past twenty years. By the end of the year, not only had his hearing been restored, he had much more vitality and he had lost 46 pounds in weight and 12 1/4 inches off his waist. He suffered no inconvenience whatsoever from the new diet, was able to come downstairs forward naturally with perfect ease, go upstairs, and take exercise freely without the slightest inconvenience, could perform every necessary office for himself, the umbilical rupture was greatly ameliorated and gave him no anxiety, his sight was restored, his other bodily ailments were ameliorated and passed into the matter of history.

Banting's Diet Prior to 1862

BREAKFAST: Bread and milk, or a pint of ea with plenty of milk and sugar, buttered toast.
DINNER: meat, beer, much bread (of which he had always been fond) and pastry.
TEA: a meal similar to breakfast.
SUPPER: generally a fruit tart or bread and milk.

Harvey's Diet Plan

BREAKFAST: 4–5 ounces beef, mutton, kidneys, broiled fish, bacon or cold meat of any kind except pork,[1] a large cup of tea (without milk or sugar), a little biscuit or one ounce of dry toast.

DINNER: 5–6 ounces of any fish except salmon, any meat except pork, any vegetable except potato, one ounce of dry toast, fruit of any pudding,[2] any kind of poultry or game, and 2–3 glasses of good claret, sherry or Madeira (champagne, port, beer were forbidden).

TEA: 2–3 ounces fruit, a rusk or two and a cup of tea without milk or sugar.

SUPPER: 3–4 ounces of meat or fish, similar to dinner, with a glass or two of claret.

NIGHTCAP: Tumbler of grog (rum): gin, whisky or brandy (without sugar) or a glass or two of claret or sherry.

1. Pork was not allowed as it was thought then that it contained starch.

2. Banting was not allowed the pastry.

Banting was delighted. He would have gone through hell to achieve all this but it had not been necessary. Indeed the diet allowed so much food, and it was so easy to maintain, that Banting said of it: "I can conscientiously assert I never lived so well as under the new plan of dietary, which I should have formerly thought a dangerous, extravagant trespass upon health.

"I am very much better both bodily and mentally and pleased to believe that I hold the reins of health and comfort in my own hands."

He goes on to wish that the medical profession would acquaint themselves with the cure for obesity so that so many men would not descend into early graves, as he believed many did, from apoplexy, and would not endure on Earth so much bodily and mental infirmity.

When Banting's booklet, in which he described the diet and its amazing results, was published, it was so contrary to the established doctrine that it set up a howl of protest among members of the medical profession. The "Banting Diet" became the center of a bitter controversy, and Banting's papers and book were ridiculed and distorted. No one could deny that the diet worked, but as a layman had published it—and medical men were anxious that their position in society should not be undermined—they felt bound to attack it. Banting's paper was criticized solely on the grounds that it was "unscientific."

Later, Dr. Harvey had a problem, too. He had an effective treatment for obesity but no convincing theory to explain it. As he was a medical man and therefore easier for the other members of his profession to attack, he came in for a great deal of ridicule until, in the end, his practice began to suffer. However, the public was impressed. Many desperate overweight people tried the diet and found that it worked. Like it or not, the medical profession could not ignore it. Its obvious success meant that the Banting Diet had to be explained somehow.

To the rescue from Stuttgart came a Dr. Felix Niemeyer. He managed to make the new diet acceptable with a total shift in its philosophy. At that time, the theory was that carbohydrates and fat burned together in the lungs to produce heat. The two were called "respiratory foods." After examining Banting's paper, Niemeyer came up with an answer to the doctors' problem. All doctors knew that protein was not fattening, only the respiratory foods—fats and carbohydrates. He, therefore, interpreted "meat" to mean only lean meat with the fat trimmed off and this subtle change solved the problem. The Banting Diet became a high protein diet with both carbohydrate and fat restricted. This altered diet became enshrined in history and still forms the basis of slimming diets today.

Banting's descriptions of the diet are quite clear, however. Other than the prohibition against butter and pork nowhere is there any instruction to remove the fat from meat and there is no restriction on the way food was cooked or on the total quantity of food that may be taken. Only carbohydrate—sugars and starches—are restricted. The reason that butter and pork were denied him was that it was thought at this time that they too contained starch.

Banting, who lived in physical comfort and remained at a normal weight until his death in 1878 at the age of 81, always maintained that Dr. Niemeyer's altered diet was far inferior to the one that had so changed his life.

Banting's *Letter on Corpulence* traveled widely. In the 1890s, an American doctor, Helen Densmore, modeled diets on Banting. She tells how she and her patients lost an average 10–15 pounds in the first month on the diet and then 6–8 pounds in subsequent months "by a diet from which bread, cereals and starchy food were excluded." Her advice to would-be slimmers was: "One pound of beef or mutton or fish per day with a moderate amount of the non-starchy vegetables will be found ample for any obese person of sedentary habits."

Dr. Densmore was scathing of those others of her profession who derided Banting's diet. She says of them: "Those very specialists who are at this time prospering greatly by the reduction of obesity and who are indebted to Mr. Banting for all their prosperity are loud, nevertheless, in their condemnation of the Banting method."

Over the following seventy years many epidemiological studies and clinical trials were conducted in several countries, and the evidence mounted. There was by the mid-1950s no doubt that the low-carbohydrate diet worked and clinical trials at the Middlesex Hospital in London had demonstrated how it worked. Doctors could now put their overweight patients on a dietary regime that enjoyed overwhelming evidence of benefit and was easy to follow and live on for life.

But it was not to be. Dieticians just couldn't seem to get their heads round the concept that eating what looked like a high-calorie diet could possibly be effective for weight loss. Or, perhaps they were afraid to lose face by admitting that they had been wrong. So they continued, myopically, to recommend that if you were overweight, it was your own fault—you were eating too much or not taking enough exercise, or both. That made life very easy for the dietitian while it ruined the life of the patient. By the late 1970s, fat was getting a bad name as a cause of heart disease (quite incorrectly as we now know). Now fat was banned for other health reasons, and carbohydrates were advocated even more strongly.

Which is why, at the start of the twenty-first century, at a time when most of us are dieting, are eating fewer calories and less fat, and taking more exercise than ever before in our history, we are getting fatter than ever before in our history.

It is no coincidence that obesity is sky-rocketing today—healthy eating advises a high-carbohydrate, low-fat diet, and the exact opposite of Banting's diet.

Not long after Banting's *Letter on Corpulence* was published the verb "to Bant" entered the language and people losing weight said they were "Banting." It remained in common parlance well into this century and one still hears it occasionally today.

Jan Freden, of Uppsala, Sweden, tells me that in Sweden, "Banting" is still the word most commonly used for dieting to achieve weight loss. So in Sweden they say: "Nej, tack, jag bantar," or "No, thank you, I am banting."

And "banting" is the noun used. We would be well advised to adopt it again.

Used by permission. * *A version of this article won the prestigious Sophie Coe Prize for the 2002 Oxford Symposium on Food History. Visit Barry Groves' Website at www.second-opinions.co.uk.*

Today, the low-carb diet is viewed by health authorities as a fad, even though low-carb has been around for over 150 years. For example, Americans ate five pounds of sugar per person per year in the late 1800s, but we are now eating 135 pounds of sugar per person per year. In our modern high-carb world, we think high is normal and normal is low. Historically, there have never been nations or groups of people who ate the excessive amounts of carbs we eat today. So low carb is actually normal carb, and high carb is the true fad.

Dr. Atkins, author of *The Diet Revolution*, discovered the benefits of a low-carb diet when trying to lose weight himself. As a cardiologist, he was able to test the effects of a low-carb diet on his patients and found that those who followed the diet lost weight easily and had marked improvement in heart health. He experienced amazing success with the low-carb diet, which did not sit well with the food and pharmaceutical industries. Dr. Atkins came under ruthless attack with outright lies and was labeled a quack. The Atkins diet was reported to be very unhealthy and extremely dangerous. Kevin remembers attending a lecture in 1977 where a well-respected physician even claimed the Atkins diet caused brain damage!

Many attempts have been made to malign Dr. Atkins and his diet even after his untimely death. Atkins died several years ago from an unfortunate accident; he slipped on the ice in front of his New York home and hit his head. Newspapers, however, including the prestigious *Wall Street Journal*, splattered the front pages with a story that Atkins was obese and died from a heart attack resulting from his low-carbohydrate diet. This false story did get retracted, eventually, but it wasn't front page news and the damage was already done; most people today believe Atkins died from his own low-carb diet.

Americans have experienced obesity and chronic disease while increasing the amount of carbohydrate and decreasing the amount of animal fat in the diet. When you follow the money, you will find that the pharmaceutical and food industries make money on carbohydrate foods. They are inexpensive to manufacture and create a market for obesity, heart, and diabetes medications. So what is the ideal amount of carbohydrate in the diet?

How much carb is too much

The total amount of carbohydrates that a person can tolerate before gaining weight or succumbing to diabetes varies from person to person due to genetics. Some may only be able to tolerate 20 grams of carbohydrate per day while others may be fine with 120 grams per day. With exercise, you may be able to tolerate a few more carbs than you would without exercising. Based on observations of thousands of patients treated with a low (or normal) carbohydrate diet, Wolfgang Lutz, MD, discovered that, for most people, the ideal carbohydrate intake is around 72 grams per day. He describes his research in his book *Life without Bread*.

Healthy people under the age of forty-five can transition immediately from a high-carb diet to a normal-carb diet without experiencing any problems, but there may be some fatigue and mood issues for the first few days due to the body overcoming the toxic effects of carbohydrates. People over forty-five and those with existing health conditions should transition slowly. If you are consuming 300 grams of carbohydrate per day, drop to 120 grams per day for at least two weeks and then work your way down from there. People with hypoglycemia and diabetes may need to transition even slower. Your carbohydrate tolerance level is the grams of carbohydrate consumed per day at which you stop losing or maintaining your weight and start gaining weight. You may experience constipation while transitioning because your previous high carbohydrate diet has left you with weak muscles in your colon and intestines, and it will take some time for them to start working again. You can use enemas to help with regularity until your muscles start to function again. If you are taking diabetes medication, you will need to work with your doctor, as those medications will need to be decreased along with your decreasing intake of carbohydrates.

The basic rules to follow with carbohydrates are:

- Never eat carbohydrate foods (grains, legumes, vegetables, and fruits) by themselves. They need to be eaten with some fat.

- Grains, legumes, and starchy vegetables should be grouped together and should be limited in the diet to no more than two servings per day.

- Fruits should be limited to no more than two servings per day.

TAKE HOME MESSAGE

1. Carbohydrates make you fat.

2. Carbohydrates play a role in most diseases today including heart disease, cancer, diabetes, ADHD, autism, and digestive disorders.

3. There is no science behind the high-carbohydrate diet.

4. The low-carb (or normal-carb) diet is not a fad.

5. Limit grains, legumes, and starchy vegetables to no more than two servings per day.

6. Limit fruits to no more than two servings per day.

7. Eat carbs with fat.

The Truth about Calories

For the past fifty years, the treatment for overweight and obesity has involved calorie counting, exercise, and behavior modification. The common belief is that a calorie is a calorie is a calorie whether it comes from fat, protein, carbohydrate, or alcohol (the only components in foods that contain calories). If you eat more calories than you exercise off, you gain weight, and if you eat less than you burn, you lose weight. It's all about calories in verses calories out. The behavior modification comes when the calorie counting and exercise don't work. It is assumed that the dieter didn't follow the diet or exercise plan, so they need psychological help to overcome their laziness and gluttony.

Is a calorie a calorie?

The "calories in versus calories out" theory is simple, and most of the diet programs out there are based on this belief. What could be easier than eating a 400 calorie bagel and exercising off those 400 calories with an hour on the elliptical machine? Calories can be measured going in and coming out. But the past fifty years tells us it isn't so simple. While we've counted calories and burned our butts at the gym, obesity rates have skyrocketed. You will even find overweight children in competitive sports programs such as diving, dancing, and swimming. Clearly the exercise isn't keeping adults or kids slim.

What is a calorie anyway?

A calorie is the amount of energy required to heat 1 kilogram of water by 1 degree Celsius in a device called a bomb calorimeter. Every gram of protein and carbohydrate take about 4 calories to heat the water while every gram of fat takes about 9 calories and alcohol takes about 7 calories. These numbers are not exact but are averaged and rounded off. We get the idea that fat is "fattening" because it requires nearly double the calories as protein or carbohydrate to raise the temperature of the water.

But does the human body burn calories in the same way that a bomb calorimeter does?

The human body is a complex system, with multiple organs, enzymes, hormones, brain chemicals, and more, and has a multitude of jobs to do. Every day, new cells are made, hormones are manufactured, and toxins are neutralized. The bomb calorimeter is essentially a tank. The food goes in and then it goes out in the form of heat. There is no manufacturing going on, and there are no thyroid glands or hormones with which to contend. Just because a gram of fat produces 9 calories in a bomb calorimeter, it doesn't mean the human body will store 9 calories from that same fat gram. In the human, calories are used for other things besides storing fat and providing energy for exercise. For example, some of the fat calories we eat will be incorporated into cells, lung surfactant, and hormones. Most of the protein we eat builds things like body tissues and enzymes. Some carbohydrate will be stored in muscle in the form of glycogen. The calories used for these purposes will not make us fat.

A lesson in physics

We cannot address the "calorie is a calorie" theory without talking about physics, because the misapplication of the laws of thermodynamics has been used to justify the calorie theory. Thermodynamics involves energy, not mass or weight. The First Law states that the energy used in doing work will be equal to the amount of work done plus the heat lost in the process. The law of conservation, which states that energy cannot be created or destroyed, only changed, is derived from this First Law of Thermodynamics.

So what does all this have to do with calories and weight gain? Essentially, it has nothing at all to do with it. What this law really says is that the calories we eat can be stored (in fat or glycogen), burned off with work (as in exercise or digesting food), or burned off as waste (as in carbon dioxide or sweat). This law does not tell us we will gain weight if we eat too much or exercise too little. But it does tell us that **not all calories will go to the fat stores in our hips because some of those calories will be used to do work and some will be discarded as waste, thus proving that calorie counting is a waste of time.**

A few health authorities recognize that the calorie theory isn't valid, but are trying to use the Second Law of Thermodynamics as justification for their beliefs. The Second Law basically states that energy will always flow from an object with a higher temperature to an object with a lower temperature. In other words, water does not flow uphill. This has absolutely nothing to do with calories in the human body and so ends our physics discussion. But here's an interesting point. Fat contains twice the energy of carbohydrate or protein, meaning that it can store more energy than a carb or protein in the same amount of space, so it is actually a good thing to store energy in the form of fat. If we stored energy as carbohydrate, we would all be extremely obese.

Count calories to gain weight

Calorie counting is futile for several reasons. First, a food eaten in June may not have the same calories as the same food eaten in December. Fruit, for instance, contains less sugar, and therefore fewer calories, at the beginning of the season than at the peak of the season. The calories in processed foods are notoriously inaccurate. Companies may change their formulas for processed foods, but continue to use old packaging. Second, there is no "one size fits all" when it comes to burning calories. Heavier people will burn more calories than slimmer people even if they are doing the exact same exercise at the same intensity. You may burn 2 calories taking a jug of milk out of the fridge while your friend burns 10 calories doing the same thing. There really is no way to be absolutely sure how many calories you are eating or how many you are burning with activity. Third, hormones, brain chemicals, the thyroid, and adrenal glands play a huge role in how we process calories. People with an under-active thyroid will store more calories as fat than someone with a properly functioning thyroid. The hormone insulin encourages the storage of fat, so if you eat foods that stimulate insulin, you will gain weight.

When you go on a low-calorie diet in an attempt to lose weight, your metabolism slows down to compensate for the decrease in energy coming in. Cells will use less energy to accomplish their tasks, and you will use less energy than normal exercising. If you normally burn 400 calories an hour on the elliptical machine while eating 2000 calories, you may burn only 200 calories on the machine while eating a 1500 calorie diet. The body wants to be in energy balance and will conserve energy going out to match the amount of energy coming in. You will become hungry and tired on the low-calorie diet, because your cells will not get the amount of energy they need to perform all their tasks. Excessive exercise will just drive up your hunger, and you will end up eating more food to compensate for the extra energy going out.

Cutting calories or busting your butt at the gym is only going to make you tired, hungry, and irritable, and that's no way to live life. So stop wasting time on calorie counting and start eating foods that encourage the release of fat from fat stores. This means eating more healthy animal fats and fewer carbohydrates. You may consume more calories eating this way, but you will lose more weight and maintain a high energy level without suffering any hunger pains.

TAKE HOME MESSAGE

1. Calories in vs. calories out doesn't work.

2. Calories are not created equal.

3. Fat calories are less fattening than carb calories.

4. Calorie counting is a waste of time.

The Cow and the Tiger

How often should you eat? Is it better to eat fewer larger meals or smaller frequent meals? Does it matter? The current trend in the marketplace is to eat a small meal every two to three hours for a total of four to eight meals a day.

Let's analyze this theory: If you want to lose weight, eat more often. Is it just us or does this sound crazy? Doesn't eating less often make more sense? This multi-munching program is fanning the flames of our chemically enhanced longing to eat more food. It's like telling a smoker to smoke more often but to take fewer puffs. So where did this ridiculous idea come from?

Meal frequency

The frequent meal theory came from the world of bodybuilding and endurance sports. A bodybuilder needs to consume a lot of calories in order to build bigger muscles; more calories than can be eaten in two or three meals a day. Extra feedings were added to keep the calories coming in. Endurance athletes like Lance Armstrong also need a lot of calories to keep up with the demands of lengthy exercise, and two or three meals just can't provide the necessary fuel. Most Americans, however, are not trying to build mass or race in the Tour de France, **so unless you are shooting for a bodybuilding title or are a super-athlete exercising all day, small frequent meals is not the program for you.**

The frequent meal theory was adopted by the weight-loss industry with claims that it prevented hunger and increased metabolism, producing greater weight loss. If you don't get hungry, you won't grab a bag of chips before dinner so you will consume fewer calories, or so the theory goes. Digestion requires a few extra calories (called the thermic effect of food), so our metabolism does speed up slightly for a short period after a meal but metabolism returns to normal within an hour. Diabetes experts also pushed the frequent meal theory claiming it would keep blood sugar levels stable, and well-controlled blood sugar keeps the weight off. But does frequent eating really stave off hunger and decrease calorie intake? Does a slight increase in metabolism for a short period of time burn enough extra calories to help you lose weight? Is frequent eating the best way to control blood sugar?

Before we answer those questions, we need to follow the money. Who benefits from Americans eating all day long? The snack food industry. They get to sell you all kinds of energy, protein, and granola bars, shakes and smoothies, chips, cookies, and crackers with processed cheese. The food industry wants you to eat as often as possible because they make money on every bite. Their goal is to sell more food more often.

Have you ever heard the phrase, "Don't spoil your appetite"? Decades ago, mothers would keep their kids out of the cookie jar between meals so they would be hungry enough to eat their dinner. Back then, obesity was not very common. Now we have snack-food vending machines in schools filled with all kinds of high-carb treats making it easy for kids to grab a snack before they get home. Dietitians receive hundreds of snack-food samples in the mail every year to hand out to their clients. The food manufacturers are essentially bribing dietitians to encourage their clients to consume more food. Since the advent of the frequent meal theory, obesity has skyrocketed out of control.

Unless you are a bodybuilder trying to gain weight,
or an Olympic Athlete, eating many meals a day is a terrible idea,
unless, of course, you're selling snack food.

Common sense tells us we shouldn't eat more often to lose weight, but what does science have to say about meal frequency?

Your body exists in one of four states.

1. **The fed state** lasts three hours after eating a meal.

2. **The early fasting state** occurs between three and eighteen hours after a meal.

3. **The fasting state** lasts from eighteen hours to two days after a meal.

4. **The prolonged fasting state** occurs after two days and continues until feeding begins again.

If you eat every three hours, you are in a fed state all day long, but if you eat two or three meals a day, you will have periods of the early fasting state. So what does your body do in these states?

In the fed state, the liver converts extra glucose (blood sugar) to glycogen and fat storage (adipose tissue). Since only a limited amount of glycogen can be stored in the liver and muscles, most of the excess glucose coming in is converted to fat. The liver also sends dietary fats and some proteins to the adipose tissue. In the fed state, you are storing fat, so while you are on the frequent meal plan, your body is in fat storage mode. Even with a slight increase in metabolism from the thermic effect of food, most people will have a difficult time losing weight when they are constantly storing fat.

The body is working all the time and needs a constant supply of energy, but blood sugar levels have to stay in a tight range to prevent coma and death. In the early fasting state, when there is no more dietary glucose coming in, the liver must manufacture glucose from non-dietary sources such as glycogen, amino acids and stored fat. This manufactured glucose is used to provide energy for essential organs in the body, such as the brain, while preserving blood sugar levels in the normal range. So, in the early fasting state, you are actually releasing fat from your fat stores. The fewer meals you eat, the more often you are in a fasting state releasing body fat.

In the fasting and prolonged fasting states, the body has to rely on fat for energy because glycogen stores are completely exhausted and protein must be spared as an energy source to produce enzymes and other substances critical for the body to function properly. Fatty acids are converted to ketone bodies, which is an alternative fuel source to glucose. The ketone bodies spare protein and keep the vital organs functioning.

Does this mean you have to starve to death in order to lose weight? No, but you do have to eat the right foods.

When you eat a high carbohydrate diet, even if you are eating "healthy" carbs, your body releases insulin. Insulin clears the sugar from your blood and puts it in the cells for energy or storage. Your blood sugar drops, causing you to get ravenously hungry. You eat again, and the cycle repeats itself. Eating small frequent meals is necessary to avoid hunger if you are on a high-carbohydrate diet. Since diabetics are put on a high-carbohydrate diet, they require more frequent meals to manage their blood sugar levels.

On a high-fat diet, you can go hours without eating and without feeling hungry because fat stays in your stomach longer and keeps you satisfied. Fat also provides a slow and steady energy supply for the body that does not require insulin. This means that your blood sugar will remain stable during the fasting state between meals so you won't get hungry. Fat is such a good source of energy that companies are now converting used fat from restaurants into an alternative fuel source!

Consider the cow and the tiger. The cow grazes all day in the pasture or feeds on grains and soybeans in the barn. Grass, grains and soybeans are all carbohydrate-rich foods, and the cow is eating several meals daily. On its high-carbohydrate, frequent-meal diet, the cow looks like a cow; large and round with no muscle definition.

A tiger, on the other hand, eats one meal every few days. He eats liver, organ meats, raw meat, fat, and muscle. This fat-munching meat-eater lives on a high-fat, low-carbohydrate diet and eats very infrequently. At the end of the day, he looks like a tiger; sleek and muscular.

The moral of the story is, if you want to look like a cow, eat like a cow. If you want to look like a tiger, eat like a tiger.

> *The moral of the story is, if you want to look like a cow, eat like a cow. If you want to look like a tiger, eat like a tiger.*

Two or three high-fat meals every day will help you release fat from adipose tissue, while several high-carbohydrate meals will cause you to store fat. We should be more concerned about what fuels the body is using to provide energy than the number of calories we are burning off with exercise or digestion. We want to release fat from adipose tissue, not deposit it. The only way to do that is with a low-carbohydrate, high-fat diet eaten no more than three times a day.

Ketosis—the friend of the body

The release of fat from adipose tissue, in the absence of excessive carbohydrates, produces ketone bodies, which are a source of energy that can be used by the body instead of glucose. When you are producing ketone bodies, you are in a state of ketosis, which is desirable because it means you are burning body fat for energy. A diet that puts you in a state of ketosis is called a ketogenic diet. When you lose weight, you want to lose fat, not lean muscle. Mild ketosis is the goal and can be measured easily with a Ketostix. It should be noted that a ketogenic diet can be very beneficial in helping someone with polycystic ovarian syndrome become pregnant, but ketogenic diets should be terminated once pregnancy occurs as they are not healthy for the fetus.

Ketosis should not be confused with ketoacidosis, a sign of poorly controlled diabetes where too many ketone bodies are produced, which lowers the pH of the blood. Mild ketosis is harmless and very beneficial for weight loss.

Fat is the preferred fuel for the body, providing a steady energy source that controls hunger and blood sugar levels so you don't experience the up-and-down sugar swings of the high-carbohydrate, low-fat diet. On the Liberation Diet you will not experience hunger pains every two hours, so you will not be tempted to down a pack of Oreos between meals. Most people think you have to have willpower to lose weight and resist that chocolate bar in the checkout lane, but willpower has nothing to do with it. If you keep eating foods that make you hungry (high-carbohydrate foods) and keep you eating all day like a cow, no amount of willpower will help you lose weight. But, if you eat healthy saturated fat and unprocessed low-carbohydrate foods two or three times a day like a tiger, you won't need willpower.

The digestive system requires a lot of energy (up to fifty percent of the body's resources) and takes energy away from other important tasks, such as thinking. If you are constantly digesting food, you are going to feel sluggish and slow like a cow. Eating less frequently allows your body to divert energy from digestion to the brain and other organs causing you to feel energized like a tiger. Productivity will increase as you begin to feel more like a human being and less like an eating machine.

Meal timing

For optimal health we need to eat two or three meals daily so we can experience periods of mini-fasts every day allowing the body to use some stored fat for energy. When should we eat these meals? Does the time matter?

You've probably been told that breakfast is the most important meal of the day, but we believe it is only important to those selling breakfast foods. If you are not hungry in the morning, skip breakfast and just eat lunch and dinner. If you are hungry when you get up, eat a hearty breakfast with plenty of animal fat, such as eggs and bacon.

If you aren't hungry in the middle of the day, eat breakfast and dinner. Do what works best for you and your schedule and don't worry about missing "the most important meal of the day."

The one thing you don't want to do, however, is eat within three hours prior to going to bed. In Japan there are very large athletes known as Sumo wrestlers who, interestingly enough, invented the thong. Now that you have that image in your mind, did you also consider that Japanese people, by nature, are not very big? The Sumo, however, is as big as a house! So what is the secret of the Sumo? How does he get so big? He eats, and goes to sleep, and eats and takes a nap. If you follow this protocol of eating and sleeping, you will also grow very large, no matter what you eat.

Eating before sleeping is a bad idea for several reasons. Your metabolism is slower at the end of the day as your body starts to wind down for rest. Eating late at night, when body cells are using less energy to do their work, means that you will store more calories as fat. Eating right before bedtime also places the body under an energy crisis. The body is ready to rest, but now has to spend half of its resources digesting food, which will prevent you from getting a good night's rest. Inadequate rest lowers serotonin levels. Serotonin is a neurotransmitter that regulates mood and appetite. When serotonin levels fall, carbohydrate cravings set in. Carbohydrates increase serotonin levels by increasing the absorption of the amino acid, tryptophan, and tryptophan increases serotonin levels. Carbohydrates will boost serotonin levels temporarily but they will also cause you to store more fat (due to the insulin response discussed in Chapter 3). When the effects of the carbohydrate meal wear off and serotonin levels fall again, you will be bombarded with more cravings and start the cycle all over.

Most Americans have rather busy schedules, meaning that some of you don't get home until 9:00 p.m. and you haven't had dinner yet. If you are in that type of situation, grab something quick, such as yogurt, earlier in the evening and skip dinner. You don't have to eat just because you missed a meal. Most Americans have plenty of "excess meals" they can access from their belly, hips and thighs.

If you go to bed with food in your belly, your body will spend the night digesting food causing you to wake up tired and looking more and more like a Sumo wrestler. When you sleep on an empty stomach, your body can rest, rebuild, and rejuvenate so you can wake up refreshed *and a little thinner!*

Fasting

If ever there was a misinformation message, it is about fasting. The food industry does not want you to fast because they can only make money when you shovel food into your mouth, so they send the message that fasting is unhealthy. But humans have been fasting for thousands of years for health, detoxification, or religious reasons.

Fasting is an excellent and very effective tool useful for healing many common disease conditions. It allows the body to rest, detoxify and heal. Instead of using energy to digest food, fasting allows energy to be used for cleansing the body of accumulated toxins, and it allows the organs to rest and rejuvenate. During a fast, the body will use stored fat to help fuel the body so you naturally lose weight while you cleanse.

Imagine bringing food into the house but never throwing out the trash. Food waste accumulates on the kitchen counters, floor, and in the cabinets. You may be able to live with that for a while, but eventually it will draw out flies and cockroaches and stink up the house. The longer it continues, the worse it gets. At some point your house becomes unlivable. When you fast, you stop bringing food through the front door and are able to take out the trash. Fasting is like spring cleaning for the body; it gives the body an opportunity to eliminate toxins and restore health to all the tissues.

> *"Take away food from a sick man's stomach and you have begun,*
> *not to starve the sick man, but the disease."*
> —E. H. Dewey, MD

The first couple days of a fast are the most difficult, especially if you are coming off a high-carbohydrate diet, because it takes the body about forty-eight hours to use up stored energy in the liver. After that initial forty-eight hours, the body switches to burning fat as the primary fuel causing wonderful side effects such as increased energy, clearer thinking, calmed nerves and absolutely no hunger. Many people confuse fasting with starvation, but they are not the same thing. Starvation occurs when all your body fat stores have been used up, forcing the body to rely on muscle and organs for energy. Most people can safely fast for up to four weeks before coming to the starvation state. Hunger will set in before that happens and is your cue to stop fasting (though it is not necessary to fast until hunger sets in). During a fast, there is generally no feeling of hunger. It is not until the body has finished cleansing that hunger sets in.

Many people today are turning to bariatric surgery and liposuction to lose weight. These procedures are not without serious risks, and they do not address the problem of obesity. They deal with the symptom rather than the cause. Fasting, on the other hand, produces the same effect as surgery or liposuction but without the complications because it deals with the cause. Stomachs will shrink to a normal size once we stop stuffing them with food, and we will eat less once we overcome food addictions. Fasting helps with both problems. It gives the stomach a chance to rest and the body a chance to clear out the toxins and overcome the addictions.

There are several different types of fasts, with the most common being water and juice fasts. With water fasts, you can only drink water (but not too much) so activity has to be limited. On a juice fast, enough energy is provided from the juice to allow a fairly normal schedule, but not intense exercise. Other beverages that can be consumed in place of juice include bone broths, raw milk and tea. We recommend these other beverages in place of juice since juice is high in sugar. If you use juice, dilute it in water to reduce the sugar content. You can also fast particular foods such as sugar, chocolate or grains to help reduce cravings for those foods.

The type of fast you go on and the number of days you spend on a fast is based on your personal needs and goals. If you have a very active lifestyle or demanding job, a water fast is probably not the best option for you unless you can take time off. Most people fast for three to five days every three to six months, but you can also fast regularly one day a week. One client lost seventy-five pounds fasting one day per week, so any level of fasting carries significant benefits. If you have existing health conditions or want to try a longer fast, we recommend that you check into a fasting clinic so you can be monitored by health professionals.

> *As a rule, probably nine out of ten well-educated*
> *Greeks and six out of ten*
> *Romans did not think twenty-two hours too long*
> *an interval between meals,*
> *which, with chatting and other pauses, lasted more*
> *than an hour and a half.*

For the first two weeks on the Liberation Diet, we recommend fasting pasteurized milk, grains and sugar. This will help jumpstart the weight loss and reduce cravings and allergies. After two weeks of eating whole, unprocessed food, you can try a water or juice type fast if you desire. It is not necessary to fast to be successful on the Liberation Diet, but it is a highly effective tool that you can take advantage of if you desire.

TAKE HOME MESSAGE

1. Eat two or three meals per day.

2. Eat breakfast only if you are hungry in the morning.

3. Do not eat within three hours of bed-time.

4. Fasting is safe, healthy, and a very effec-tive weight loss tool.

5. If you get hungry between meals, you are not eating enough fat.

MSG: The Stealth Additive

The food industry has a problem; they can't make money on real food, but manufactured food doesn't taste very good. The solution is food additives, which are generally inexpensive and improve the taste, texture, look and feel of a food to entice customers to buy over and over again. Naturally, the food industry loves them because they put more money in their pockets. By far, the most popular additive is monosodium glutamate, or MSG.

The Japanese used a seaweed called Kombu in some dishes to enhance the flavor. In 1908, Dr. Kikunae Ikeda discovered that the ingredient behind the incredible taste-enhancing properties of this seaweed was glutamate, an amino acid. A year later, Ikeda hooked up with his friend Dr. Saburosuke Suzuki to form the company Aji-nomoto and, together, they took this miracle flavor enhancer, in the form of monosodium glutamate, to the world.

MSG is a boon to the food industry because it can make even bland, low-fat, diet food taste like a gourmet treat and it takes the "tin" taste out of canned food. Cow pies would even taste good with MSG. Soldiers in World War II had a taste of MSG in Japanese army rations and were amazed at how good their rations were compared to the American rations. Since the war, American food companies have used more and more of this miracle additive in everything from in-fant formula to canned soup. Most, if not all, processed food contains MSG even if it isn't labeled.

Have you seen the potato chip commercial that says, "Bet you can't eat just one"? Don't take that bet because you'll lose. Those chips are loaded with MSG, which is so good, it's addicting. The food industry is giving you an addicting substance while the diet industry is telling you to use willpower. If willpower was all you needed, it wouldn't be hard to quit smoking and it wouldn't be hard to eat just one chip. The reason MSG is so valuable to the food industry is that it keeps you, the consumer, coming back for more food. It's the MSG that draws you to your favorite restaurant, fast food, and snack.

MSG may be great for the food industry, but is this addictive substance good for our bodies?

MSG studies

The FDA granted MSG a Generally Recognized as Safe (GRAS) standing in 1959. Since then, the glutamate industry has conducted dozens of studies to "confirm" the safety of MSG in an attempt to discredit independent researchers who have found MSG to be detrimental to health.

In 1968, Dr. John W. Olney discovered that, in mice, MSG damaged the neurons in the retina of the eye, the hypothalamus, and other areas of the brain. Younger mice suffered more toxic effects than older mice and developed short stature, obesity and reproductive problems. At that time, large amounts of MSG were put into baby foods. Mothers must have been happy to see their precious little tykes eating so well, but Olney was concerned that feeding MSG at such an early age would cause problems with growth and brain function due to the effects of MSG on the hypothalamus.

The medical community ignored Olney's findings so he petitioned the FDA to have MSG removed from baby food. The glutamate industry fought back with an impressive study showing no health problems in animals given extremely high doses of MSG. It turns out that since the animals vomited from such high doses, they actually ingested negligible amounts of the stuff. Olney also found out that the animals were anesthetized with a drug that blocks the uptake of glutamate into the neurons and protects the hypothalamus from damage. The FDA based their conclusions on a completely invalid study. Because most of the officials had financial ties to the glutamate industry, they dismissed Olney's concerns about the safety of MSG. The FDA continues to rely on industry-funded research to keep MSG in GRAS status.

But what does independent research show?

Glutamate is a common excitatory neurotransmitter that plays a role in memory, sensory perception, cognition, motor skills, and orientation in time and space. The brain requires glutamate to function properly, but too much glutamate will "excite" or stimulate neurons to death. Think of an overly stimulated child having a melt down. Glutamate stimulates neurons in the hypothalamus, a tiny piece of brain that regulates hormone balance and therefore indirectly controls the adrenal glands, thyroid and reproductive glands. It also controls appetite, sleep and waking cycles, and our biological clock. A properly functioning hypothalamus is essential to achieve or maintain a healthy weight.

Most obesity experiments are conducted on rats, but rats are not normally obese, so they have to be fattened up. The number one model used to induce obesity in rats is MSG. If you want a fat rat, you feed the rat MSG from infancy. If MSG makes rats fat, what do you think it will do to you?

The January 2006 issue of the *European Journal of Clinical Nutrition* contained a study concluding that MSG damages the hypothalamic regulation of appetite. A 2005 study in the *Anales de la Real Academia Nacional de Medicina* demonstrated that MSG affects the hypothalamic control of various hormones and also increases appetite. And if you're still not convinced, the June 2005 issue of *Nutrition* found that adding MSG to the standard American diet increased food intake and oxidative stress. MSG is also being used to induce Type II diabetes in rats. These studies are just a sampling of the science discrediting the FDA and glutamate industry belief that MSG is safe.

So, we have an obesity epidemic with rising rates of Type II diabetes and a food additive that is in most everything we eat that causes obesity and diabetes. Could there possibly be a connection? The science, so far, seems to support this hypothesis. Following are three ways MSG can cause obesity:

1. Recent research has demonstrated that adequate sleep is important for weight control. One of the effects of MSG on the hypothalamus is that it disrupts your sleep cycle.

2. Can you down a whole dish of Kung Pao Chicken with fried rice and be starving to death an hour later? The addictive nature of MSG keeps you coming back for more food because it disrupts appetite control. Not only are you eating more food, you are eating more often (like a cow), which is a recipe for obesity.

3. Thyroid and adrenal hormones accelerate the release of fatty acids from adipose tissue, which is essential for weight loss, but MSG destroys the hypothalamus, which indirectly controls the release of these hormones.

Exciting brain cells to death can also lead to Alzheimer's, Parkinson's, attention deficit disorder, autism and more. Along with our increased use of MSG, we are seeing an increase in learning disabilities in children.

MSG is not safe

It is interesting to note that the food industry is feeding you glutamate while the pharmaceutical industry is manufacturing drugs that block glutamate to use as treatments for Alzheimer's and other neurological disorders. Also, as Asians adopt a more Westernized diet in place of their traditional diets, they are experiencing a rise in obesity and diabetes. Traditional Asian cuisine is lower in glutamates than the Western diet. If they used MSG, it was derived from a natural source, whereas now, MSG is chemically manufactured.

Glutamate in whole, unprocessed food is harmless, unless eaten to excess, as in a high-protein diet, because it is bound to other substances. When foods, proteins in particular, are manufactured or processed, they develop a free, unbound form of glutamate that contains carcinogens and other harmful compounds. Free glutamate is much easier to get into cells than bound glutamate. MSG is not always labeled because there are a multitude of ingredients that contain hidden MSG, and the FDA believes it is okay to put this poison in your food without telling you. **But if MSG is safe, as the glutamate industry wants you to believe, why are they trying to hide it?** Following is a list of ingredients where MSG may be hiding (from www.truthinlabeling.org)

ALWAYS CONTAIN MSG

Glutamate	Monosodium glutamate	Monopotassium glutamate
Glutamic acid	Yeast extract	Hydrolyzed protein
Calcium caseinate	Sodium caseinate	Yeast food
Hydrolyzed corn gluten	Gelatin	Textured protein
Yeast nutrient	Autolyzed yeast	Natrium glutamate

OFTEN CONTAIN MSG OR CREATE
MSG IN PROCESSING

Carageenan	Natural pork flavoring	Bouillon and broth
Natural beef flavoring	Stock	Whey protein concentrate
Whey protein	Whey protein isolate	Flavor(s), flavoring(s)
Maltodextrin	Citric acid	Natural chicken flavoring
Ultra-pasteurized	Barley malt	Pectin
Protease	Protease enzymes	Anything enzyme modified
Enzymes anything	Malt extract	Malt flavoring
Soy protein isolate	Soy sauce	Soy sauce extract
Soy protein	Soy protein concentrate	Anything protein fortified
Anything fermented	seasonings	

Disodium guanylate and disodium inosinate are expensive food additives that work synergistically with MSG, so their presence suggests that the product contains MSG. Low-fat and fat-free milk products that include milk solids will contain MSG as well.

The best way to avoid MSG is to eat whole, unprocessed foods and avoid processed foods. At restaurants, ask the waiter if there are foods that do not contain MSG. You can use naturally brewed soy sauce. Eden and San J are a couple of brands that should be available most everywhere.

TAKE HOME MESSAGE

1. Most processed food contains MSG even if it isn't labeled.

2. MSG increases your appetite.

3. MSG makes you fat.

4. Avoid processed food and ask restaurants which foods are MSG free.

5. Use naturally brewed soy sauce.

With a Grain of Salt

Salt, the much-maligned essential nutrient, has been a precious commodity for thousands of years. People who lived by the sea enjoyed salty fish and sea vegetables, and those who lived inland burned salty marsh grass and sprinkled the ashes on their food. Our word "salary" dates back to the time when Roman soldiers were paid in salt instead of money. Even Jesus talked about the "salt of the earth" and told his followers to be "salt and light." God said "salt is good" and commanded the Israelites to use salt with Old Testament offerings. In history, salt was a valuable commodity. So why is there so much controversy about using it today?

In the early 1900s, studies seemed to connect high blood pressure to salt intake, so doctors and dietitians began to warn their patients about consuming too much salt. Since then, salt has been discouraged on the stove top and banned at the dinner table. Many packaged and processed foods advertise "low sodium" on their labels, and we even have salt-free salt substitutes. But is it a good idea to restrict salt in the diet? The Japanese consume about twice as much salt as Americans, yet they live longer and suffer less heart disease.

Sodium and chloride have several important functions in the body. Hydrochloric acid, found in our stomachs, is made from the chloride component of salt and is necessary for the digestion of meat. Chloride also activates the enzymes needed to digest carbohydrates and keeps the brain and nervous system functioning properly. Sodium is important for nerve impulse conduction and muscle relaxation and contraction. Together, sodium and chloride regulate fluid and acid-base balance and keep the adrenal glands functioning. If you are tired all the time, you may need to eat more salt.

How much salt do we need?

Because salt is the most common source of sodium in the diet, the two are often used interchangeably. When your doctor tells you to cut back on salt, he or she is really telling you to reduce sodium in your diet. High blood pressure is blamed on the sodium component of salt. Humans only need about 200 mg of sodium to survive, but it would be impossible to consume such a small amount since sodium is found in virtually every food. The typical diet contains about 2,000 mg to 5,000 mg of sodium per day. Generally, salt excretion is equal to the amount we eat, so the kidneys do an excellent job of keeping sodium levels constant. The Center for Science in the Public Interest (CSPI), however, is campaigning to lower the sodium recommendations from the current government-recommended 2,400 mg per day to a mere 1,500 mg per day. These are the same people who removed healthy animal fats from the diet and replaced them with deadly trans fats. With their anti-saturated fat campaign "in the public interest" came skyrocketing rates of obesity and increased heart disease, cancer and diabetes.

If CSPI has their way with salt, we can expect more health problems to develop in healthy people. Perhaps a better name for CSPI would be Center for Sleazy Pharmaceutical Interests since their campaigns lead to the use of more medication to combat the health problems caused by the campaign. But we digress...

As individuals, we all need different amounts of salt, so it is foolish to put everyone on a low-salt diet. Salt restriction has been shown to lower blood pressure in people with low levels of the kidney hormone renin, but salt raises blood pressure in people with high levels of renin. More recent studies have not found a relationship between salt intake and high blood pressure in most people. In fact, salt restriction may cause high blood pressure and heart disease in some people.

Good salt, bad salt

Today there are many different forms of salt from which to choose. Most of the salt consumed is refined salt, but trendy sea salts, kosher and coarse salts are on the rise. Does it matter which kind of salt you use?

Pure, unrefined salt from the sea contains about 82% sodium chloride, about 14% macro-minerals such as magnesium and close to eighty trace minerals including a natural form of iodine. Due to its mineral content, sea salt is grey in color and a bit moist. Refined salt on the other hand contains 100% sodium chloride along with aluminum based anti-caking agents, and an unnatural and potentially toxic form of iodine that has to be stabilized by dextrose (a sugar). The dextrose causes the salt to turn purple, so a bleaching agent is used to make the salt white.

Magnesium is one of the best minerals around to lower blood pressure and prevent heart attacks. Natural iodine is better absorbed than the potassium iodide added to refined salt and is necessary to keep the thyroid gland functioning properly. We only need small amounts of trace minerals, but without them, we would be unable to maintain good health. Sea salt can help replace those vital minerals. Refined salt lacks the nutrition of sea salt, and some of the additives can be harmful. Aluminum, for instance has been linked to Alzheimer's disease.

Clearly, salt is essential in the diet, and the kind of salt you eat makes a difference in terms of health; it may even be more important than how much salt you eat. We recommend using unprocessed sea salts containing natural iodine such as Celtic Sea Salt or Real Salt. Read the ingredient list because many refined sea salts on the market have similar packaging to unrefined sea salt—sort of like the wolf in sheep's clothing. Avoid processed foods, which are loaded with refined salt and other harmful ingredients, but don't be afraid to use good sea salt while cooking or at the table. We liberate you to sprinkle a little sea salt on your favorite dish; your taste buds will thank you and your heart may tick a little longer.

TAKE HOME MESSAGE

1. Avoid refined salt and processed foods.

2. Use unrefined sea salt such as Celtic Sea Salt or Real Salt brands.

3. It's okay to use real sea salt in cooking and at the table.

Water Damage

Nutritionists have been recommending eight cups of water a day for at least twenty years, but none of them can tell you where they got this advice. They can't point you to any studies or scientific evidence because there are none. Even nephrologists (kidney doctors) don't have a clue as to why people are told to drink so much water. So do we really need eight cups of water a day? If you're into extreme sports or nursing a baby, maybe; but for average folks, the answer is no.

To replace water lost from exercise, sweat, urine, lungs, and skin, an average person needs about 2,000 ml of water; the equivalent of eight cups daily. However, you don't need to get all eight cups from a water bottle. We produce about 1½ cups from metabolic processes, and the remaining 6½ cups is divided equally between food and beverages. Food has a pretty high water content. For example, an egg is 75% water and a cucumber is 99% water, and food also provides vitamins and minerals. So, we only need about three to four cups of water or other non-alcoholic beverages per day.

Water myths

Several myths are floating around to get people to drink more water. Dieters are advised to drink water before they eat to curb appetite, so water is marketed as a weight loss tool. But what happens if you drink before eating? Hydrochloric acid is secreted into the stomach when we eat, and its purpose is to facilitate the digestion of food. Drinking water will dilute this acid, thus impairing digestion and opening the door for heartburn, acid reflux, and other digestive upsets; not a good trade-off for a couple pounds of weight loss.

If you look at the rising rates of obesity that parallels the rising intake of water, it becomes clear that water is an ineffective tool for weight loss.

While dieters are getting soaked, health authorities are telling the general public that the thirst mechanism cannot be relied upon because dehydration has already occurred by that time. This is absolute nonsense. Our thirst mechanisms are triggered with a 2% rise in blood concentration, but dehydration does not occur until a 5% rise in blood concentration, giving us plenty of time to down some fluids before we become dehydrated. The thirst mechanism works well in most people, but may not function properly in the elderly, so as you get older, you may have to set up times to drink.

Another myth is that dark urine is a sign of dehydration. As the volume of urine decreases, urine does become darker; however, urinary volume varies greatly from one individual to another. Urine color is also influenced by certain foods, B vitamins, medications, and artificial colors, so dark urine does not automatically indicate dehydration. If you're urinating less than normal and your urine is dark, then you may need to get more fluids, but you don't have to chug a jug of water just because your urine is dark.

Health enthusiasts claim that eight or more cups of water a day is necessary to flush out toxins. Water will help to remove toxins after the liver and kidney have done their jobs just because water is the medium that carries and transports everything in the body. Excess water will not increase the release of toxins, but it will increase the loss of vital minerals such as potassium, sodium, magnesium, and calcium, especially if the increased water intake is accompanied by a high-carbohydrate diet. Not too long ago, a radio station had a contest to see who could drink the most water. The winner would receive a Wii. A young mother won, but ended up dead from hyponatremia. She lost too much sodium because she drank too much water in too short a time. Many athletes suffer from hyponatremia as well because they drink water to replace fluids, but do not replace electrolytes like sodium and potassium. One of Kevin's personal training clients was an editor of a metropolitan newspaper. In her town, a college-aged rower died of a heart attack. Kevin suggested the cause was water intoxication, and sure enough, after some investigation, the editor reported that the death had been caused by too much water.

Health authorities tell us to drink plenty of water to prevent constipation, but a high water intake actually causes constipation. Excess water increases urinary volume, which causes more potassium to be excreted. Potassium helps the body re-absorb water, and the loss of potassium dries out the stools causing constipation. It's the potassium not the water that keeps stools moist.

Kidney stones and degenerative bone disease can be caused by too much water due to the loss of calcium. Muscular disorders such as fibromyalgia and fatigue may result from the loss of magnesium and calcium. If you've ever watched a prize fight, you may have noticed the boxers take a sip of water and then spit it out. Swallowing the water would flush the calcium and magnesium out of the body, and the boxers need those minerals to stay in the game. Other conditions related to mineral loss include heart disease, heart attack, angina, arrhythmia, and unstable blood pressure.

How much fluid do you need?

Water is not a safe nutrient. It is essential, but we don't need eight cups a day. If you have a dog, you will notice that the dog will drink a little more in hot weather and a little less in cold weather. You could put eight bowls of water out for the dog, but he will only drink the amount he needs; no more, no less. Just like the dog, we need a little more water in hot and humid climates (including saunas) and a little less in cold climates. Fever increases the need for water by about a cup a day. Nursing mothers need more water to compensate for the fluid lost in milk, and athletes need more than sedentary folk.

Following are some common sense rules to follow when it comes to water:

- Drink when thirsty (it doesn't have to be water; milk, broth and tea work, too).

- Drink a little during strenuous exercise (just add liquid minerals to the water).

- If you urinate more than five times a day or have to get up at night, you are drinking too much.

- Don't drink within an hour of eating. If you need a beverage with meals, broth or raw milk are the best options.

Just don't drink to your health!

TAKE HOME MESSAGE

1. You don't need to drink eight glasses of water a day.

2. Drink when thirsty.

3. Don't drink within an hour of eating.

4. Choose lacto-fermented beverages, tea, broth, milk, or water with added minerals.

Exercise Myths

Just as birds are built to fly, humans are built to exercise. We are perfectly suited to lift, carry, push, pull, squat, press, jump, walk, and run. Exercise is essential for all humans because it strengthens muscle and bone, makes us feel good, and helps maintain our independence to a ripe old age. Even comatose patients in the hospital receive exercise to keep their joints and muscles limber. But what impact does exercise have on weight loss?

The common belief is that exercise is absolutely essential for anyone who wants to lose weight. Exercise is touted as the be-all-end-all of weight loss, enabling you to eat whatever you want so long as you burn it off at the gym. But the truth is that no amount of exercise can overcome poor eating habits. Exercise plays a very small role in weight loss compared to diet; it's an 80/20 ratio where diet accounts for 80% of the weight loss and exercise accounts for 20%. Yet many people hiring personal trainers just want to work on exercise; they don't think they need to change their diet. As more and more gyms and fitness centers spring up and more people start exercising, obesity rates rise instead of fall.

For those of you celebrating right now, we are not saying you don't have to exercise. We highly recommend exercise for all its health-giving benefits such as improved strength and muscle tone, strong bones, a healthy heart, reduced stress, energy, stamina, confidence, improved digestion, and better sleep. Exercise also helps the lymphatic system operate, enables us to participate in fun activities, and helps us enjoy life to a higher degree. Both diet and exercise are important for good health, but the good news is you don't have to bust your butt at the gym every day to achieve it.

Exercise types

There are several different forms of exercise, and it's important to include all of them in your routine. Every week, you want to include aerobic exercise, strength training, and flexibility training.

Aerobic exercise, or cardiovascular training, strengthens the heart and develops stamina and endurance. The more you give your heart a workout, the more you are able to do and the farther you are able to go because you build up endurance. Examples of aerobic activities include swimming, walking, running, biking, step aerobics, and dance. Most sports involve some sort of aerobic training, so exercise doesn't have to be boring. Even gardening and housework provide a workout for your heart. Get 20 to 60 minutes of aerobic activity at least three days a week. You do not have to do 90 minutes as recommended by the Food Guide Pyramid and Dietary Goals. They recently increased exercise recommendations since their low-fat, high-carbohydrate diet isn't working to prevent obesity. If you exercise too much, you will just end up with a ravenous appetite and overeat, sabotaging any efforts to lose weight.

Strength training provides a broad range of benefits, including increased metabolism so you burn more calories when not exercising, increased lean body mass, improved posture, and increased bone density. Years ago, strength training involved gym machines or free weights, but now there are other options such as stability balls, tubes, bands, bars, and medicine balls to make the workouts more fun. The focus of strength training is evolving to include balance and core training (working on the stomach muscles). Functional fitness is a type of strength training that improves one's ability to perform daily activities such as bending, lifting, and reaching—things that become more difficult as we age. Strength training should be done for at least 20 minutes two to three days per week.

Flexibility training is important to keep muscles stretched out and lean. The more flexible you are, the fewer injuries you will have. Flexibility allows full range of motion in joints, allowing you more freedom in movement so you can engage in a variety of activities.

Pilates and yoga are examples of flexibility exercises, and it's always a good idea to stretch out before and after a workout. Flexibility training can be done two or three days a week.

The amount of time you spend on each exercise session and the number of days you exercise depends on your goals and your schedule. If you are an athlete in training, you will require more exercise than the average person. If you want to build muscle you may need more strength training, and if you are looking to build up endurance, you may require more aerobic activity. Start near the bottom because it's much easier to work your way up with exercise than to get an injury and have to cut down on exercise.

Annette recently got involved in competitive swimming, so she needs a little more aerobic training to build endurance. She does a 90-minute swim workout with a coach three days a week, and if the weather is good, she will take a 30-minute walk a couple of non-swimming days. She also enjoys about 20-minutes of Pilates two or three days a week and 20-minutes of strength training two or three days a week. The number of days depends on her schedule and what her swim coach has her doing that week in the pool. Too much muscle will make it difficult for Annette to swim because fat floats and muscle sinks, so she takes it easy on the strength training. Annette is particularly fond of the stability ball and free weights.

Kevin enjoys weight training so he spends 45 to 60 minutes three to four days per week in the gym. For aerobic activity, Kevin prefers a little variety in the great outdoors; he will ride a bike, play basketball or take a walk, demonstrating that you don't have to do the same thing every day to get healthy.

Getting active

It really doesn't take much exercise to improve your health. Getting started is usually the hard part, so **pick an activity or several activities that you enjoy**. Do not force yourself to do something you hate because you will just stop exercising. If you don't like the gym, don't buy a gym membership. For example, Annette will not go to a gym. She just doesn't enjoy working out on machines, so a gym membership would be a waste of money for her. However, she loves to swim and likes her swim coach so it's easy to get her suit on and brave the snow (not that she gets much snow in her neck of the woods but you get the idea) to go work out. She does her own weight training program at home with the stability ball and uses Windsor Pilates videos. **Do what works best for you.** If the gym is your thing, join a gym; if you like the outdoors, take up jogging or biking. Don't forget to count gardening, housework and playing with your kids as exercise. It all adds up.

Once you choose an activity, **get a nice workout suit that looks good on you.** You will be more motivated to exercise if you look good. You will want to choose the activity first because that will determine what type of outfit you need. If you're swimming, a jogging suit won't help much. It may get you from the car to the pool, but you won't be able to get far once you're in the pool. You may be more comfortable in Capri style pants doing Yoga or Pilates than with short shorts, but shorts may work better for tennis.

Start slow. You don't need to do 100 push-ups on your first day, and you don't want any injuries. If you can only do five minutes, do five minutes and pat yourself on the back. At this stage, you are just trying to develop the habit of exercise.

We, of course, recommend that you get a personal trainer, especially to help with strength training. At a minimum, you would want a trainer to set up a workout you can do at home and change it every six weeks. The benefits of a trainer include:

- **Accountability.** With a trainer, you either train or you lose money.

- **Consistency.** You are more likely to keep up with regular exercise if you have to report to someone.

- **Injury prevention.** A trainer can show you how to do the exercises properly and correct poor form as well as set you up with an appropriate workout so you don't get hurt.

- **Individualization.** Exercise is not one-size-fits-all, and a trainer has the expertise to design a program tailor made for you with exercises you enjoy.

- **Progression.** The more you exercise, the more efficient you become at it and the less effective the workout becomes. A trainer can alter your routine periodically to improve your fitness level and prevent boredom.

Exercising with a personal trainer can be very rewarding. Studies have shown that people work out more vigorously with a trainer than they do on their own. Just be careful about the nutritional advice they dispense, as most trainers preach the low-fat, high-carbohydrate diet. Naturally, we would be happy to develop an exercise program that will work for you and you won't have to listen to the low-fat dogma. If you would like to try personal training, call our toll-free number at 1-800-327-3010 and someone will assist you in getting started. You can also log onto our online fitness program at www.LiberationFitness.com to enjoy personal training in the privacy of your home at a very modest cost.

If you can't afford a personal trainer right now, just start walking. It's a great exercise anyone can do, and it doesn't require any special equipment; just a good pair of athletic shoes. You can also use a video. The best way to find a video is to rent several at your local library or movie rental place. When you find a few you like, go buy them. With videos, it's best to have more than one to keep boredom at bay.

If time is a factor for you, we recommend spending less time working out and a little more time in the kitchen preparing healthy meals. The weight will come off much faster, and you'll feel a lot better. Turn cooking into an aerobic activity with some music. Just swing your hips and move your feet in place as you chop and stir.

Exercise should be fun and natural without consuming all your time and energy.

TAKE HOME MESSAGE

1. Exercise plays a small role in weight loss.

2. You don't have to spend a lot of time exercising.

3. Choose an activity you enjoy.

4. Hire a personal trainer to help you with proper technique.

The Result of Bad Advice

The switch from whole, unprocessed food to fake food has had a disastrous impact on human health. As we have decreased saturated fat, total fat, and cholesterol in our diets to make room for more grain, fiber, and sugar, we have experienced a significant rise in obesity and chronic disease. How can we possibly think that continuing on this path is going to improve our health when the past forty-plus years has demonstrated the detrimental effect of this new-fangled diet on human health?

Obesity

Obesity is certainly forefront in the minds of many Americans today. There is a plethora of information about the dangers of this health crisis and innumerable methods and programs to combat obesity, but we can see from general observation that they aren't working. If anything, they are adding to the crisis! We need a different solution, based on accurate information, if we are going to win the battle of the bulge.

Obesity is defined as:

"An abnormal accumulation of body fat that frequently results in a significant impairment of health."

(Obesity begins at a body mass index of 30 and overweight begins at a BMI of 25)

By definition, obesity affects more than just your dress size. Carrying around excess weight increases your risk for high blood pressure, Type II diabetes, heart disease, stroke, gallbladder disease, osteoarthritis, sleep apnea and other respiratory conditions as well as breast, endometrial and colon cancers. Depression is also a common side effect of obesity. If a debilitating disease or chronic depression isn't bad enough, obesity also accounts for an estimated 112,000 deaths annually. The costs associated with obesity are pretty hefty, too. Annually, Americans spend about $90 billion on medical treatments and about $30 billion on weight loss books, products, and services.

The term "abnormal" is also rightly used in that obesity is anything but normal.

Look at any picture containing a group of Americans from the 1950s or earlier and count the number of overweight people. You will most likely have to look very hard to find just one. Kevin was in Washington D.C. recently and visited the Arlington National Cemetery. Inside the visitors center he noticed a wide panoramic picture of President Eisenhower's motorcade en-route to the presidential swearing-in ceremony circa 1952. The parade route was lined with thousands of people, yet Kevin was unable to find anyone who looked overweight or obese. But, as he looked around the room where he was standing, he had a hard time finding someone who wasn't overweight. Today as you walk down the street or in the mall, you will notice many overweight people. Without the old picture to have as a point of reference, being overweight gradually becomes—normal.

We don't need to be rocket scientists to conclude that Americans are not genetically predisposed to becoming obese. History reveals that overweight and obesity have never been the norm for our nation. Obesity is a new phenomenon that has only developed within the last forty years, though there are some who want you to believe beer bellies and holster hips are normal and inevitable as if we are evolving into a larger species.

Epidemic is defined as:

"Occurring suddenly in numbers clearly in excess of normal expectancy; applied also to any disease or health-related event."

Obesity was practically non-existent in the late 1800s and grew only slightly worse until the mid-1900s. Around 1960, obesity rates began inching upwards, skyrocketing out of control between 1980 and 2004 when rates doubled in the U.S. and Australia and tripled in the United Kingdom. In the U.S., two out of three adults suffer from overweight or obesity, and our children are getting fatter, too. Obesity increases as underdeveloped nations become civilized and abandon their traditional diets and as developed nations forge ahead with new technologies and modern food preparation methods. We are clearly experiencing a global obesity epidemic that will have a catastrophic impact on the world as insurance rates rise and medical costs soar.

Obesity statistics			
	1960–1962	1976–1980	2001–2004
6–11 year olds	4.2%	6.5%	17.5%
12–19 year olds	4.6%	5.0%	17.0%
20–74 year olds	44.8%	47.4%	66.0%

Many view obesity as a disease that must be treated, particularly the pharmaceutical industry that stands to profit from their weight-loss drugs. Obesity is being touted as a hereditary disease creating victims that have no control over the situation and, therefore, must rely on medicine as the only *sensible* way to battle the problem. More and more people are turning to surgeries and drugs in an effort to control their weight problem, especially since Medicare and other insurance companies now cover weight loss. Surgeries and drugs only work if you stick to a very strict diet and they generally come with unpleasant side effects, so in the long term, the cost far outweighs any benefits. Not everyone is a candidate for a drug or surgical procedure, so we can't count on these treatments to take a bite out of obesity.

Prevention is usually the best bet, but obesity is becoming a political platform as health organizations, government agencies, celebrities, and politicians implement all kinds of programs to prevent waistlines from expanding further. Once a cause becomes politicized, there is a lot of busyness, but no real results. To make matters worse, all of these programs give the same advice; eat less fat and saturated fat, eat more grains, fruits, and vegetables, and exercise more. We have been following this advice for the past forty years while our bottoms have bulged out of our pants. One definition of insanity is doing the same thing over and over but expecting different results. We've had forty years of insanity so far. How much longer are we going to cut the fat before we realize it's not working?

Insanity is ...

... doing the same thing over and over but expecting different results!

Most of you reading this book know what we mean. You've tried the low-fat, high-carbohydrate diet and spent hours in the gym only to gain more weight. You may have jumped from Weight Watcher's to Jenny Craig to LA Weight Loss and nothing works, at least not long term. Some of you have endured a verbal lashing from your doctor because of your "lack of willpower." Instead of blaming the diet advice that doesn't work, you get blamed for not sticking to the diet.

The obesity epidemic is spurred on by the food and pharmaceutical industries that stand to make a profit from our expanding waistlines. Our fast-paced "I need it now" society doesn't help, but ultimately, we each have to take responsibility for ourselves. Human nature wants to avoid conflict and shift blame to someone or something else because it's easier. While there are forces out there that make losing weight difficult, we have a choice and a responsibility to reverse this obesity epidemic. We need to do this not only for ourselves, but for our loved ones and future generations.

The obesity epidemic in America is:

- Partly the fault of businesses that profit from it.
- Not a disease.
- Not hereditary (meaning it's not something you can't control).
- Something we can overcome.
- Something for which we must take responsibility.

Chronic Disease

In the early 1900s, Americans could expect to live about 47 years. At that time most deaths were due to infectious diseases such as tuberculosis and influenza. Today, our life expectancy is up to 80 years, but we are suffering from chronic diseases of civilization such as heart disease, cancer and diabetes. Increased life expectancy and improved sanitation partly account for the shift from infectious disease to chronic disease, but our lifestyle choices play a more significant role.

**Diseases of Civilization (also called Lifestyle Diseases)
are defined as:**

"Diseases associated with the way a person or group of people
live that appear to increase in frequency as countries become
more industrialized and people live longer."

"They include Alzheimer's disease, atherosclerosis, cancer, chronic
liver disease, chronic obstructive pulmonary disease, Type II
diabetes, heart disease, chronic renal failure, osteoporosis, acne,
stroke and depression."

What you eat, do, and breathe has a huge impact on your health.
It matters if you smoke, exercise, eat right, or breathe in chemicals.
These lifestyle choices will determine whether you live to a ripe old
age still able to do what you want, or whether you spend your last
years or decades in a nursing home with some stranger giving you
baths and changing your diapers.

Most lifestyle diseases take time to develop, so we refer to them
as chronic rather than acute. Infectious diseases are acute in that they
have a rapid onset and you either recover in a matter of weeks, if not
days, or you die. Chronic diseases have a slow onset of several years or
decades and usually end up putting you six feet under only after they
have taken away years of your independence.

Chronic disease results from years of inactivity, processed food,
smoking, stress, exposure to chemicals, and following the politi-
cally correct but scientifically inaccurate nutritional advice dis-
seminated by the government and health organizations. With the
exception of the chemicals and some degree of stress, these are things
you have complete control over, or will after you finish this book.
No one is forcing you to down a package of Oreos, watch hours of
television, or light a cigarette. Chronic lifestyle diseases are abso-

lutely preventable, and sometimes reversible, if you eat the right foods, move your body, and learn to relax, so it is mind-boggling to find the following definition of chronic disease in the medical literature.

Medical view of chronic disease:
"A disease that can be controlled but not cured."
CCHS

Why would wise lifestyle choices not be a cure for these diseases, since the opposite is their cause? If these diseases can be prevented, why do a growing number of people suffer from them?

The first heart attack (myocardial infarction) was reported in 1921 and accounted for about 3,000 deaths annually by 1930, but this increased to over 700,000 deaths by 2006.

Reported Deaths from Heart Attack in the U.S.

- 1921 – 1
- 1930 – 3,000
- 2006 – 700,000+

Deaths from all forms of heart disease went from 10% in 1900 to 50% last year. What happened in the last century to create this heart disease epidemic that kills one out of two people in the U.S.?

Heart disease is not the only killer out there. Cancer deaths have been on the rise over the past century despite all the latest diagnostic tests, chemo, radiation, and surgeries. Cancer is the second leading cause of death, killing one out of four Americans every year, even though millions of dollars are pouring into organizations like Race for the Cure.

Diabetes is also on the rise and is one of the leading causes of disability, with side effects such as kidney failure, blindness, nerve damage, amputated limbs, and more. Diabetes treatments range from insulin and oral medications to a fifty-percent carbohydrate diet, yet none of these things are very effective at treating diabetes for any length of time and they certainly don't offer any cures.

More and more Americans are suffering from mental illness and dementias as well. Depression could be the second big killer after heart disease by the year 2020 and is increasing faster in children than any other age group. More and more children are also being diagnosed with bipolar disorder, ADHD, and autism.

Alzheimer's is a devastating form of dementia first diagnosed in 1901. Currently, complications from Alzheimer's kills one out of eight Americans annually, and the number of people suffering from this disease is growing. Parkinson's disease is on the rise, too. We are experiencing an exponential increase in diseases that hardly existed 100 years ago.

Americans are plagued with the epidemic of chronic lifestyle disease, and scientists are looking for ways to treat these diseases. But wouldn't it be better to find a cure through ways to prevent or reverse these life-destroying diseases? As with the obesity epidemic, government and health authorities continue to give out the same nutritional advice—eat less fat and saturated fat and eat more grains, fruits, and vegetables. Diet is usually the last resort after drugs and surgery, even though diet plays a role in the development of the disease. Again, the definition of insanity is doing the same thing over and over but expecting different results. As we continue to follow the same advice, the death rate from chronic disease continues to rise. We've followed this advice for over forty years. How much longer do we just sit back and accept chronic disease as inevitable, normal, and acceptable?

Heart disease, cancer, diabetes, Alzheimer's and other chronic diseases were almost unheard of at the beginning of the twentieth century when medical technology was in its infancy. But now, as we make advances in diagnostic, surgical, and pharmaceutical technology, the death rate continues to increase. What changed between

1900 and 2006 that modern technology can't fix? So far, technology has just given rise to newly invented diseases like osteopenia and the disease of high cholesterol, putting millions of extra Americans on medication.

If our goal is to just treat symptoms but never cure the disease, we are on a dead-end street. It seems like the last thing our health system wants to do is give information that would actually cause a person to become completely well. We think you deserve to know how to prevent these diseases so you can live a full life while enjoying your family, friends, and independence.

Get Liberated

Good health is your responsibility, not your doctor's or the government's. The choices you make will have a huge impact on your short- and long-term health. In America, you have the freedom to accept or reject treatments and choose for yourself how to best stay healthy. You don't have to go along with the status quo—a path that is clearly paved with despair. You can be liberated, free to be healthy and fit. We have shown you how all the diet advice dispensed over the past forty years has actually caused obesity and chronic disease. Now we want to put you on the fast track to good health and a slimmer physique, so you can enjoy life to the full.

Weston A. Price

Weston A. Price was a well-respected dentist in the early 1900s and was widely published in peer review journals. He became the first head of research for the National Dental Association. Unlike other dentists, Price was not content to just fill cavities and perform root canals. He believed that tooth decay was a symptom of some underlying disease or nutritional deficiency, so he spent twenty-five years studying the relationship between root canals and disease. Often, he was able to cure the underlying disease by removing the root canal. This led him on a quest to find out how tooth decay could be prevented, thereby eliminating the need for fillings and root canals and improving the health of the patient.

His quest led him to many remote and isolated peoples. He studied the Swiss, Gaelics, Eskimos, North American Indians, Melanesians, Polynesians, African tribes, Aborigines and Peruvian Indians. Price noted significant differences in the nutritional content of the diets of primitive and isolated peoples compared to the modernized diets of Western civilization. He was especially intrigued by the fact that primitive peoples had nice wide jaws, straight teeth and no tooth decay. They also did not suffer from diseases of modern civilization such as heart disease and cancer. Price even brought his camera along to take pictures of these remarkably healthy people.

When analyzing the diets, Price discovered significant differences in the amount of fat-soluble vitamins and minerals consumed by primitive peoples compared to modern civilizations. They also ate whole foods without refined sugars, salt and flour. Primitive peoples adopted food preparation techniques that not only improved the nutritional content of the food, but made them easier to digest.

Following is a list of characteristics found in traditional diets:

1. The diets of healthy, non-industrialized peoples contain no refined or denatured foods or ingredients, such as refined sugar or high fructose corn syrup; white flour; canned foods; pasteurized, homogenized, skim, or low-fat milk; refined or hydrogenated vegetable oils; protein powders; artificial vitamins; or toxic additives and colorings.

2. All traditional cultures consume some sort of animal food, such as fish and shellfish; land and water fowl; land and sea mammals; eggs; milk and milk products; reptiles; and insects. The whole animal is consumed—muscle meat, organs, bones, and fat, with the organ meats and fats preferred.

3. The diets of healthy, non-industrialized peoples contain at least four times the minerals and water-soluble vitamins, and ten times the fat-soluble vitamins found in animal fats (vitamin A, vitamin D and Activator X) as the average American diet.

4. All traditional cultures cooked some of their food but all consumed a portion of their animal foods raw.

5. Primitive and traditional diets have a high content of food enzymes and beneficial bacteria from lacto-fermented vegetables, fruits, beverages, dairy products, meats, and condiments.

6. Seeds, grains, and nuts are soaked, sprouted, fermented, or naturally leavened to neutralize naturally occurring anti-nutrients such as enzyme inhibitors, tannins, and phytic acid.

7. The total fat content of traditional diets varies from thirty percent to eighty percent of calories but only about four percent of calories come from polyunsaturated oils naturally occurring

in grains, legumes, nuts, fish, animal fats, and vegetables. The balance of fat calories is in the form of saturated and monounsaturated fatty acids.

8. Traditional diets contain nearly equal amounts of omega-6 and omega-3 essential fatty acids.

9. All traditional diets contain some salt.

10. All traditional cultures make use of animal bones, usually in the form of gelatin-rich bone broths.

11. Traditional cultures make provisions for the health of future generations by providing special nutrient-rich animal foods for parents-to-be, pregnant women, and growing children; by proper spacing of children; and by teaching the principles of right diet to the young.

Price also noticed that these same primitive peoples would develop poor jaw structure, tooth decay, and chronic disease if they adopted a modernized diet. It was the diet that mattered, not their location or amount of isolation. Something in the primitive diet promoted a health and vitality that was lacking in Western civilization.

Unfortunately, most doctors and dietitians are unfamiliar with the work of Dr. Price. After World War II, medicine shifted from an emphasis on nutrition and prevention to an emphasis on drugs and surgeries. Nutritionists were no longer qualified to "treat" people so they were prevented from performing any meaningful research because they were unable to observe the effects of diets or nutrients on people. Research was demoted to what could be discovered in a laboratory or test tube.

The Liberation Diet is in line with the discoveries of Weston A. Price. We believe we should eat foods that nourish the body and the soul, providing every opportunity for excellent health and long life.

Special thanks to Sally Fallon and The Weston A. Price Foundation, a nonprofit charity dedicated to restoring nutrient-dense foods to the human diet through education, research and activism. We encourage all our readers to visit their Website at www.westonaprice.org.

Know Your ABCs

Vitamins were unknown before the twentieth century, but certain foods were associated with the cause or prevention of various diseases. In the 1700s, it was discovered that citrus fruits could prevent scurvy, a disease caused by vitamin C deficiency, but it was not until the 1930s that vitamin C was identified as the protective factor. Dr. William Fletcher, in 1905, discovered that eating unpolished rice prevented the disease beriberi. He concluded that the husk of the rice kernel must contain some substance that protected against the disease. Five years later, a Japanese scientist discovered the B vitamin thiamin to be the protective element in the rice husk.

Throughout history, primitive man has adopted various methods of food preparation that give strength to the body and produce healthy offspring. The early American Indian, for example, developed a process whereby dry maize (corn) is soaked and cooked in a five-percent lime solution to separate the outer hull from the grain making it easier to grind the grain and improving the flavor and aroma of the finished product. This process also prevented the disease pellagra, which is a disease of niacin deficiency. The soaking made the niacin in the corn available for the body to use. The Indians didn't know anything about niacin, but they knew that maize wasn't fit for consumption without the soaking. Vitamin research is barely 100 years old and, ironically, correlates with the advent of processed foods such as pasteurized milk, vegetable shortening, and refined grains—foods that have been stripped of much of their vitamin content. Traditional cultures instinctively knew what to eat to stay healthy, and science is now backing up those instincts.

Fat-Soluble Vitamins

The fat-soluble vitamins are A, D, E and K, and they require fat to be digested and absorbed. Dr. Price found that the diets of isolated primitive peoples provided about ten times the amount of fat-soluble vitamins as the Standard American Diet. Our low-fat diet coincides with increased rates of obesity, heart disease, cancer, diabetes, osteoporosis and infertility, which are partly due to the lack of fat-soluble vitamins. If you take the fat out of your diet, you take these vitamins out as well. Dr. Price found that these fat soluble "activators" were essential in the diet and enabled the body to utilize all other vitamins and minerals.

Vitamin A

Vitamin A was discovered by E.V. McCollum somewhere between 1912 and 1914. He found that a diet containing butter would cause rats to grow fat and healthy, but rats fed the same diet containing olive or bleached cottonseed oil (Crisco) instead of butter would be sickly. He named the substance in butter "fat-soluble factor A." This was a landmark study because it demonstrated that **butter, a saturated fat, contained a substance critical for human health that was not in olive oil or Crisco.**

Vitamin A is usually labeled as retinol and is found only in animal fats such as butter, whole milk, egg yolks, liver and organ meats, seafood and fish liver oils. Dr. Price found that vitamin A from animal foods is necessary for the body to utilize protein, minerals and water-soluble vitamins. Other functions of vitamin A include:

- Proper vision.
- Growth and reproduction.
- Proper bone development.
- Immune function.
- Detoxification of pollutants, antioxidant.
- Tissue repair.

- Maintenance of mucous membranes and skin.
- Thyroid function.
- Production of stress and sex hormones.

Vitamin A is essential for life but surrounded with controversy and confusion. As little as 5,000 IU of vitamin A per day has been linked to osteoporosis and bone fractures. Dr. Price did not observe this in primitive peoples who were consuming 50,000 IU of vitamin A, so what's the deal? Most of the studies carried out on vitamin A use a synthetic form. Natural vitamin A is found in foods that are also high in vitamin D. Vitamins A and D seem to work together preventing each other from becoming toxic. Each also increases the need for the other. Vitamin D increases the need for vitamin A and vitamin A increases the need for vitamin D, so it's essential to get these nutrients in the right balance, something easily done if eating real food. The synthetic vitamin A studies did not contain vitamin D, and that is why they revealed toxic outcomes. Synthetic vitamin A is added to many fabricated foods such as margarine and breakfast cereals, and it is also added back to reduced-fat milks to replace the vitamin A lost when the fat is taken out.

These studies have initiated a fear of vitamin A, so most supplements contain carotenes, the pro-vitamin form of vitamin A. Carotenes, beta carotene being the most common, are found in dark-green leafy, orange, and yellow vegetables and fruits and can be converted to vitamin A when needed. Vegetarians, therefore, claim that humans can get all the vitamin A they need from carotenes, making animal sources of true vitamin A an unnecessary addition to the diet. Unfortunately, this conversion process is limited in infants, children, diabetics, and people with poor thyroid function (which includes about half the population). Fat is essential for this conversion to take place, so it is also limited in people consuming a low-fat diet, yet another good reason to butter your vegetables. According to the latest research, it appears to take 21 units of beta carotene to make 1 unit of vitamin A. Additionally, 80 to 90 percent of vitamin A is absorbed from food but only 5 to 50 percent of beta carotene is absorbed. You'd have to eat an awful lot of salad to come close to meeting your vitamin A requirements with beta carotene.

Most people believe that carotenes are safe and non-toxic. Sure, they may turn your skin orange if you take too much, but they won't do any permanent damage. That is not true, according to the research. Beta carotene can actually induce cancer. In people with low blood levels of vitamin A, beta carotene may increase those levels somewhat, but beta carotene can also reduce levels of activated vitamin A in certain tissues. The mechanism used by beta carotene to reduce active vitamin A is the same as that used by dioxins (environmental toxins) to cause cancer. Excess beta carotene combined with polyunsaturated fat seems to increase oxidative stress and create compounds that destroy vitamin A, which leads to poor health and the development of diseases such as cancer.

This does not mean that we should avoid carotenes, as they are powerful antioxidants and low levels are associated with vaginal candidiasis. However, carotenes do not perform all the functions of vitamin A and, therefore, should not be relied on to meet your vitamin A requirements. We should also not consume a diet high in polyunsaturated fat to minimize the interaction between beta carotene and these fats.

Other things that interfere with the conversion of carotenes to vitamin A or the absorption of vitamin A include:

- Antibiotics, laxatives, fat substitutes, and some medications.
- Strenuous physical exercise.
- Excessive consumption of alcohol.
- Excessive consumption of iron (especially from "fortified" white flour and breakfast cereal).
- Excessive consumption of polyunsaturated fatty acids.
- Zinc deficiency.
- Even cold weather.

The best way to get plenty of vitamin A in the diet is to eat animal fats found in egg yolk, liver, shellfish, fish liver oil, butter, and whole milk from animals that are allowed to graze. Milk from confined cows and eggs from caged chickens does not contain adequate levels of vitamin A. This is due to a combination of the animal receiving feed that is lacking in vitamin A (green pastures are rich in the vitamin), stress experienced by the confined lifestyle, and lack of sunlight. Stress depletes the body of vitamin A in both humans and animals. Notice the difference in color between butter from a confined cow and butter from a grass-fed cow. The yellow color of the grass-fed butter contains significantly more vitamin A.

Getting your vitamin A from animal fats ensures that you will also get vitamin D to prevent vitamin A toxicity. Don't avoid carotene rich fruits and vegetables, but do be sure to eat them with plenty of butter.

How much vitamin A?

FDA regulations allow food processors to **label carotenes as vitamin A**. For example, if you look at a food label for tomato paste, it will say that two tablespoons of paste contains 10% of your vitamin A requirement (about 500 IU). Tomato paste contains carotenes, not vitamin A, so if you calculate the 21 to 1 conversion of carotenes to vitamin A, the paste ends up providing a maximum of 24 IU or only 0.5% of your vitamin A requirement. You need carotenes and vitamin A to be truly healthy, so get your vitamin A from animal foods and your carotenes from fruits and vegetables.

(Pastured, Organic and Conventional)

Vitamin D

With the industrial revolution came the bone disease known as rickets. The rise of rickets was eventually traced to the fact that people were leaving the outdoor farm life to live in polluted cities where they spent most of their time indoors. There seemed to be something magical about sunlight.

It turns out that the human body can make vitamin D out of cholesterol when the sun hits our skin. Summer sun between the hours of 10:00 a.m. and 2:00 p.m. is best for making vitamin D, and the lighter your skin, the more vitamin D you make. Sunscreen, clothes, and smog inhibit the vitamin D making effect of sunlight. Vitamin D can also be found in animal foods such as butter, egg yolk, cod liver oil, fatty fish, liver and organ meats, chicken skin, and seafood. The vitamin D we make from sunlight or get from animal foods is called cholecalciferol or vitamin D3.

Cholecalciferol makes the pre-hormone calcidiol, and calcidiol makes the steroid hormone calcitriol, the active form of vitamin D. Calcitriol has the following functions:

- Regulation of calcium, phosphorus, magnesium, iron, and zinc absorption.
- Regulation of calcium balance.
- Stimulation of bone cell mineralization (if calcium intake is adequate).
- Antioxidant.
- Protection against diabetes.
- Protection against auto-immune disorders such as multiple sclerosis, rheumatoid arthritis, and Crohn's disease.
- Anti-carcinogen.
- Production of estrogen.
- Weight control.

Vitamin D has come to the limelight recently, and studies are underway to demonstrate its many benefits. Research is showing that our paltry 400 IU recommendation for vitamin D intake is far below what's needed for health, with scientists now recommending up to 4,000 IU daily. It is, however, critical to get adequate calcium with vitamin D. A lack of calcium will cause the D to take calcium out of the bones.

Because vitamin D has such a wide range of benefits and because we have practically eliminated vitamin D rich foods and sunlight from our daily lives, it is a good idea to have your vitamin D levels checked. When getting a blood test to check for vitamin D status, make sure the test is for calcidiol or 25(hydroxyvitamin)D, not for calcitriol. Calcitriol levels fluctuate too much to be useful as an indicator of vitamin D status, and it can be manufactured by the kidney in response to low vitamin D levels. Optimal vitamin D blood levels are around 45 to 50ng/ml.

There is another form of vitamin D known as ergocalciferol, calciferol, or vitamin D2 that is derived from fungus such as mushrooms or yeast. When D2 is added to foods or used in supplements, a hormone is taken from the fungus and then irradiated in the laboratory to produce the D2. Ergocalciferol, which does not exist in the human body in detectable amounts, is the most common form of vitamin D added to foods and supplements. Cholecalciferol is more potent than ergocalciferol because the latter is converted to substances that are foreign to the human body in addition to calcitriol.

Rickets is on the rise again because we don't allow children in the sunlight without sunscreen and we have all but eliminated animal fat from the diet of our children. Polyunsaturated vegetable oils and monounsaturated olive oil also interfere with our ability to use vitamin D, yet we are told to increase these oils in our diets.

The best way to get vitamin D is to eat animal fats and take high vitamin cod liver oil (see the Supplement Chapter). Getting out in the midday sun without sunscreen is a good idea and a great mood booster, but the sun is not a reliable source of vitamin D for everyone, so don't depend on it. Once again, real food contains other nutrients such as vitamin A and calcium that work with vitamin D. Supplements should contain natural vitamin D from fish liver.

Vitamin E

Vitamin E is the name given to eight different compounds; alpha, beta, gamma and delta tocopherols and tocotrienols. Alpha tocopherol is the most common form. Vitamin E has the following functions:

- Antioxidant.
- Circulation.

- Protection for vitamin A.
- Tissue repair and healing.

Vitamin E is a powerful antioxidant that works with selenium and zinc to prevent heart disease and cancer. The best dietary source of vitamin E is wheat germ oil followed by nuts, seeds, and green leafy vegetables. Vitamin C will restore vitamin E in the body to its normal antioxidant state, so they are best eaten together.

In America, vegetable oils are the most commonly added fat in the diet. We are told to avoid saturated fats like butter and coconut oil and use soybean and canola oil instead. Most processed foods contain a combination of corn, soybean, cottonseed, and canola oils. The unprocessed forms of these oils contain vitamin E, and the processed oils usually have vitamin E added back. Our need for vitamin E increases as we increase our consumption of vegetable oils, because these oils are unstable and go rancid quickly. Vitamin E steps in to prevent oxidation of these oils, thus decreasing free radical formation and preventing cell membrane damage.

Vitamin E supplements come in natural and synthetic forms. If you see "l" (lower-case L) or dl-alpha tocopherol on the label, it is synthetic. D-alpha tocopherol is the natural form. The synthetic form is not as potent as the natural form, but is more toxic, so avoid synthetic vitamin E—foods with that "l" (lower-case L) on the label. Most supplements also only contain alpha tocopherol, but it is best to get a mix of alpha, beta, gamma and delta tocopherols.

Vitamin K

There are three forms of vitamin K. K1 is found in plant foods such as seaweed and dark green leafy vegetables, K2 is synthesized by bacteria and found in fermented foods and grass-fed animal fats, and K3 is a synthetic form that is not readily available for the body to use. Bacteria synthesis of vitamin K in the gut provides about half of our vitamin K needs.

Vitamin K1 is mostly involved with blood clotting and along with K2 protects against glutamate toxicity. Dr. Price discovered a substance called "activator X" that has the following functions:

- Utilization of minerals.

- Protection against tooth decay.

- Support for growth and development.

- Involved in normal reproduction.

- Anti-carcinogenic.

- Synergistic with the other "fat soluble activators" vitamins A and D.

- Protection against calcification of the arteries (reduces risk for heart disease).

- Major component of the brain.

Recently, it has been determined that "activator X" is vitamin K2. Humans can convert vitamin K1 into vitamin K2, but we still need a dietary source of K2 to be truly healthy. The more vitamin K2 we consume, the lower our risk for heart disease—another reason to include good old-fashioned healthy animal fats in the diet. Fermented foods such as natto, cheese, and sauerkraut are also excellent sources of vitamin K2 or "activator X." The best supplemental source of K2 is high-vitamin butter oil.

Antibiotics and diseases that interfere with the healthy bacteria in our gut limit vitamin K production.

Coenzyme Q10

Coenzyme Q10 is sometimes referred to as "vitamin Q" and it is fat soluble and essential to life, so it warrants a discussion. Every cell in the body requires coenzyme Q10 to produce energy, with the heart using the majority of this nutrient to keep pumping. Coenzyme Q10 also functions as an antioxidant and is used to treat cancer and heart and gum diseases. The best food sources are animal products. People taking statin drugs to lower cholesterol need supplemental coenzyme Q10 as the drugs block its formation in the body. It is this effect on coenzyme Q10 that causes the debilitating side effects of statin drugs.

Water Soluble Vitamins

B vitamins

The B vitamins are involved in energy metabolism, formation and development of blood cells and other metabolic actions and promote healthy skin, eyes, liver, hair, muscle tone, cardiovascular health, and nerves. B vitamins are found in whole grains, fresh fruits, vegetables, nuts, legumes, seafood, and organ meats, and they can also be produced by intestinal bacteria.

We will just single out two of the B vitamins: B12 or cobalamin, and B6 or pyridoxine. The usable form of vitamin B12 is found only in animal foods and is needed for fertility and to promote normal growth and development. Soy advocates claim that soy provides B12, but it actually has a B12-like substance that does not function like B12. Eating unfermented soy foods actually increases your need for the vitamin.

Vitamin B6, also called pyridoxine, is found mostly in animal foods and is necessary for the proper functioning of over 100 enzymes. Vitamin B6 is extremely heat sensitive, so the best sources are raw milk and meat, foods that have been eliminated in the Standard American Diet. Excessive amounts of the B vitamins thiamin and riboflavin interfere with the function of B6. One of the problems with refined grains is that they are enriched with thiamin and riboflavin, but not pyridoxine. Diabetes, heart disease, and nervous disorders have been linked to a deficiency of B6.

Vitamin C

When we think of vitamin C, also known as ascorbic acid, we usually think of a cure for the common cold, but vitamin C has many crucial functions in the body including:

- Tissue growth and repair.
- Adrenal gland function.
- Lactation.
- Formation of collagen.
- Wound healing.
- Antioxidant.
- White blood cell activity.
- Protection of LDLs (low density lipoproteins) from free radical damage.

Some animals are able to synthesize vitamin C from glucose, but humans lack an enzyme necessary for this conversion. However, glucose does have an impact on vitamin C absorption because they compete with each other for the same absorption pathway. In other words, they are both trying to flag down the same taxi, but only one can fit in the taxi at a time. The taxi driver likes glucose better, so he chooses to take glucose for a ride instead of vitamin C. Glucose also impairs the ability of the kidneys to reabsorb vitamin C, increasing the amount of vitamin C lost in the urine. The only diet that supplies excessive glucose is a high-carbohydrate diet such as the Food Guide Pyramid diet. **The more carbohydrates in your diet, the more vitamin C you need.** The amount of vitamin C in our tissues may depend more on how much glucose is in the diet than how much vitamin C we are taking in.

High protein diets, aspirin, oral contraceptives and alcohol also decrease vitamin C levels in the body. Sources of vitamin C include citrus fruits, berries, peppers, parsley, Brussels sprouts, broccoli and other fruits and vegetables, raw milk and organ meats.

Vitamin research shows us that we need animal foods in the diet to be truly healthy. Vegetarian diets cannot provide the same level of nutrition as animal-based diets because several key nutrients are found only in animal foods. Every nutrient, including vitamin C, can be supplied by some animal food. The vitamin story also demonstrates the superiority of a low-carb diet for human health and longevity.

TAKE HOME MESSAGE

1. Animal foods provide all the nutrients you need.

2. Eat full-fat animal foods.

3. If you eat real food, you won't have to worry about getting the right balance of nutrients.

Milk Matters

One of the most bizarre tales in the battle to keep people thin and healthy is the story of milk. Real milk is the super-healthy, disease defying food that has nourished mankind since the beginning of time, but is now tainted with controversy and even *banned in some states in America!* So, if you want to stir up some trouble, start talking about milk.

Some think milk is totally unsuitable for human consumption after the age of two while others believe milk is the perfect beverage. The diet and fitness industry is loving milk right now because of research showing that calcium promotes weight loss, but some doctors argue that milk causes allergies, asthma, and a host of other health problems. Then there are wars about the fat content of milk with most health authorities recommending skim milk over whole milk. The most recent debate is between organic milk and milk containing antibiotics and rBGH (recombinant bovine growth hormone).

Before the invention of skim milk and rBGH, the debate was between raw milk and pasteurized milk. Raw milk, also known as unpasteurized or real milk, is the only milk that should be given the label "milk." Pasteurized milk with all its additives and processing **is not milk, but a processed food or "fake milk."** Back in the old days, most everyone drank raw milk. It was believed to be a healthy food, especially for children. Today most people believe that they will develop a food-borne illness if they drink raw milk, and they believe pasteurized milk is perfectly safe and does not interfere with the nutritional quality of the milk. But are our beliefs about raw and pasteurized milk grounded in truth?

Another industrial waste product

The story begins with the War of 1812 when Americans were cut off from their whiskey supply in the British West Indies. This was a time when more and more people were living in cities that were crowding out farms and pasture. But American saloons needed a supply of whiskey to keep their customers happy, and greater and greater numbers of city dwellers needed a supply of milk.

Soon, every city had at least one distillery that extracted starch and alcohol from grains, leaving an acid refuse known as distillery slop or swill. Distillery owners would keep cows nearby and feed them the distillery slop, and swill milk was born. The slop did nothing for the nourishment or health of the cow but it did cause them to produce an abundant supply of milk. Since the cows receiving the slop were unhealthy, the milk was also defective—so much so that it could not be made into butter or cheese, but could be sold only as milk.

The poor distillery cows were forced to live out their short lives, usually less than a year, in severely confined quarters that were never cleaned. The air was polluted from the distillery as well as from cow excrement. Pails used to collect milk were generally dirty, and the workers collecting the milk did not wash their hands, cough in their sleeves, or practice any kind of sanitation. If the slop sent the cows to an early grave, what effect did it have on humans?

Infant mortality rose alarming high with the advent of distillery dairies and about half of all deaths were attributed to the slop milk, which was blamed for diarrhea, scarlet fever, diphtheria, and tuberculosis. Clearly, something had to be done. At this time, two theories about the cause of illness were circulating among scientists and doctors.

The debate begins

Claude Bernard's *milieu interieur* theory stated that illness was caused by a weakened immune system. If you gave the body proper nourishment, it would be able to fight off any infection and heal itself. Louis Pasteur's *germ theory* stated that infectious diseases were caused by germs and could only be cured with drugs. The germ theory gained in popularity since it was a boost to the pharmaceutical industry. These theories set the stage for the debate between raw and pasteurized milk. Those who sided with Bernard believed the production of milk should be regulated so as to minimize harmful pathogens while keeping intact the immune-building properties in the milk. Others who sided with Pasteur believed that all bacteria should be destroyed.

By the late 1800s, most people realized that swill milk was a problem and a solution was way overdue. Dr. Henry Coit believed the production of milk should be controlled; cows should be allowed to graze and eat an appropriate diet, clean pails should be used to collect milk, and farm workers should be clean and free from illness when collecting milk. Coit initiated the certified raw milk movement that supports Bernard's theory.

Nathan Straus, a businessman and philanthropist, campaigned to pasteurize milk to make sure it contained no harmful bacteria. Strauss was so committed to his pasteurization campaign that he actually sold pasteurized milk below cost in an effort to convince people to use pasteurized milk over raw milk. Strauss did admit, however, that pasteurization would not be necessary if one could get pure, fresh milk from a healthy cow. Strauss was camping out with Pasteur's germ theory.

The last swill milk distillery closed its doors in 1930, but the debate between raw and pasteurized milk continued on with the pasteurization camp gaining more and more ground. Most of the milk sold in stores was pasteurized, but small, local farms provided certified raw milk to consumers who wanted it. Pasteurization was good for big business because it increased the shelf life of the milk, which meant more money coming in. It was much easier and less expensive to pasteurize dirty milk than to clean up, certify, and monitor the dairies.

Smear tactics

After World War II, the debate heated up with the pasteurization proponents hurling outright lies against raw milk. One such lie appeared in a 1945 article in the *Coronet* titled, "Raw Milk Can Kill You," by Robert Harris, MD. This article told of a town called Crossroads, USA, where one out of every four persons in the town suffered from brucellosis, or undulant fever, caused by raw milk. The author later admitted that this town never existed and the story was completely fabricated. This was just the beginning. The media jumped on the pasteurization bandwagon and spread lies and half truths in an attempt to convince the public that raw milk was dangerous and deadly and pasteurized milk was the only safe milk to drink.

Even today, the FDA and health police are biased against raw milk. A May 1983 campylobacter outbreak in Pennsylvania was blamed on raw milk even though CDC's *Morbidity and Mortality Weekly Report* admits that cultures taken from the raw milk did not contain any campylobacter. Organic Pastures, a raw milk dairy in California that has sold over 40 million servings of raw milk without a single case of illness, was blamed for an outbreak of E. coli in four children in 2006. The dairy was shut down while over 2,000 tests were performed on the entire dairy operation. Not a single pathogen was found, but state health officials continue to report that Organic Pasture's raw milk caused illness. It just so happens that all four children also ate raw spinach or sushi, which was most likely the cause of the food poisoning.

The largest recorded outbreak of salmonella occurred between June 1984 and April 1985 and sickened over 200,000 people and caused 18 deaths. The cause was **pasteurized milk.** For some reason, the CDC did not issue a specific *Morbidity and Mortality Weekly Report* for this outbreak, but the incident is reported in the *FDA Consumer* and the *Journal of the American Medical Association*. Most recently, three people have died and one woman miscarried due to a 2007 outbreak of listeria from **pasteurized milk** in Massachusetts. It barely got mentioned in national news.

Most food-borne illness is due to contaminated produce, poultry, beef, eggs, and seafood. Raw milk only causes problems if sanitary conditions are not met or if the cows are inappropriately tended. Raw milk from grazing, grass-fed cows that is collected under sanitary conditions is perfectly safe. Pasteurized milk does not guarantee safety, but you won't hear that from the FDA or health authorities with an agenda to pasteurize all milk.

Current trend in milk production

The current trend in dairy farming is to "go big." Cows are confined to concrete pens and fed grains (which contain aflatoxins that can be passed into the milk) and soybeans instead of fresh grass. Grains lower the pH of the cow's stomach, opening the door for E. coli contamination in humans. Normally, E. coli cannot survive in an acid environment, and a cow's stomach is not as acidic as a human stomach. When the pH of the cow's stomach is lowered due to grain consumption, it gives rise to resistant E. coli. In other words, E. coli adapts to the acid environment and becomes immune to it. When humans eat foods contaminated with resistant E. coli, they get sick because the acid environment in their stomach that would normally kill the bacteria is no longer acidic enough.

As dairies grow in size, machines do most of the work from milking to cleaning so farmers don't know their animals. Everything is done to increase milk production with little thought to the quality of the milk or the life of the cow. Unfortunately, dairies that don't "go big" are at risk for failure because the price of milk is fixed by big business, not by farmers. They are forced to cut costs wherever possible. As milk production increases, milk quality decreases.

Problems with pasteurized milk

Pasteurization allowed for milk to be retrieved from a cow in California and shipped to a store in New York, so it was a real boon to the dairy industry. If you are going to drink swill milk, you definitely want it to be pasteurized to prevent illness. But what does pasteurization do to the milk? Is it really better to drink pasteurized dirty milk than fresh raw milk from a clean, grass-fed cow? The FDA and health authorities would have you believe the nutritional content of pasteurized milk is exactly the same as the nutritional content of raw milk.

Heat destroys or alters many substances, including amino acids, enzymes, and vitamins. The pasteurization of milk has these effects:

- Alters amino acids.

- Destroys enzymes completely. When enzymes are consumed with food, they help the digestive process and preserve body enzyme stores allowing the pancreas to rest. Enzymes in milk help digest the butterfat, lactose and proteins. Milk allergies may be due to the effects of pasteurization rather than the components in milk.

- Destroys significant amounts of vitamin C, lowers content of some B vitamins and inactivates vitamin B6.

- Alters lactose making it more readily absorbable, meaning sugar goes to the bloodstream quicker requiring the need for insulin.

- Causes the unsaturated fatty acids in milk to go rancid, which can lead to free radical build up in the body.

- Alters the mineral components in milk such as calcium, magnesium, phosphorus, chlorine, potassium, sulfur, and trace minerals, making them less available for the body to use.

- Causes milk to putrefy instead of sour. Sour milk is actually good for you, but putrid milk is not.

Clearly, pasteurized milk is not as healthy as raw milk, as long as that raw milk comes from a clean, healthy cow that is allowed to graze in a pasture. The perception that raw milk is not safe is so far from the truth, it couldn't be further from the truth! *Raw milk is uniquely safe* in that it contains multiple bioactive components that can reduce or eliminate populations of pathogenic bacteria. These bioactive components are almost completely de-activated when milk is pasteurized resulting in a very unsafe product.

Destruction of Bioactive Components by Pasteurization

Component	Breast Milk	Raw Milk	Pasteurized Milk	Infant Formula
B-lymphocytes	X	X	inactivated	inactivated
Macrophages	X	X	inactivated	inactivated
Neutrophils	X	X	inactivated	inactivated
Lymphocytes	X	X	inactivated	inactivated
IgA/IgG Anti-bodies	X	X	inactivated	inactivated
B12 Binding Protein	X	X	inactivated	inactivated
Bifidus Factor	X	X	inactivated	inactivated
Medium-Chain Fatty Acids	X	X	reduced	reduced
Fibronectin	X	X	inactivated	inactivated
Gamma-Inter-feron	X	X	inactivated	inactivated

Lactoferrin	X	X	inactivated	inactivated
Lyxozyme	X	X	inactivated	inactivated
Mucin A/Oli-gosaccharides	X	X	reduced	reduced
Hormones & Growth Factors	X	X	reduced	reduced

Scientific American, December 1995; *The Lancet*, Nov. 17, 1984

Raw milk also contains lactic-acid-producing bacteria that protect against harmful bacteria. With the government's efforts to sterilize the food supply, these healthy bacteria, also known as probiotics, have been destroyed, leaving more room for the growth of harmful bacteria. The healthy bacteria can actually prevent pathogenic bacteria from causing problems should any pathogens inadvertently contaminate the milk.

Homogenization

Homogenization followed closely on the heels of pasteurization for several reasons. Back in the old days, milk was delivered to doorsteps in the early morning and the quality of the milk was judged by the amount of cream sitting at the top; the more cream, the better the milk. To gain, or steal, customers from competitors, dairies would leave a free sample of milk. Housewives would compare the amount of cream between the free sample and their regularly delivered milk. If the sample contained more cream, the housewife would cancel the regular dairy and switch to the new dairy. Homogenization put an end to competition because it dispersed the cream so no one could see how much (or how little) cream was in the milk.

Pasteurization kills bacteria and white blood cells in raw milk leaving the dead particles to form an unsightly sludge at the bottom of the jug. (Yes, you do drink dead bacteria when you drink pasteurized milk.) Homogenization disperses this sludge throughout the milk so it can't be seen by you, the consumer.

As pasteurized milk traveled long distances, the cream would rise to the top and some customers would get mostly cream and others would get mostly skim milk. Homogenization made it possible to distribute the cream evenly between customers, but it wasn't readily accepted. People liked the cream on the top so they could judge the quality of the milk. In an effort to convince consumers to drink homogenized milk, the industry had some salesmen drink homogenized milk and un-homogenized milk. The salesmen then vomited up the milk and put the curds in a jar. Homogenized milk had smaller curds, so the salesmen could now show the housewife that homogenized milk was easier to digest. He would just whip out his two jars of vomit and demonstrate the size of the curds. Whether people believed the smaller curd size made a difference or whether they just got tired of opening their door to vomit, the scheme worked and by the 1950s, most milk was homogenized.

Homogenization has been blamed for heart disease, but there are some flaws in the theory, so we can't say for sure that it does cause heart disease. But one thing homogenization does do is alter the fat globules so that there is more protein incorporated into each globule. This may be one reason so many people have milk allergies.

Non-fat dry milk powder

With homogenized milk, it's impossible for consumers to tell how much fat is in the milk. Before government interference, the butterfat content of milk was between 4 and 8%. Now the highest butterfat content in processed milk is 3.5%. Due to our fear of fat, more people are drinking skim and low fat milk in an attempt to prevent heart disease. When the fat is taken out, something has to be added to give milk a creamy white texture; that something is non-fat dried milk powder. Since the addition of non-fat dried milk powder to skim and low-fat milks is an industry standard, it does not have to be labeled on the milk carton. All skim and low-fat milks contain non-fat dried milk even if it isn't listed in the ingredients.

Non-fat dried milk is high in protein and vitamins, so one would think it is a healthy addition to the milk, but it actually does more harm than good. The production of non-fat dried milk produces cancer-causing nitrates and oxidation of cholesterol. Normal cholesterol found in food is harmless, but when cholesterol is oxidized, it causes plaque build up and atherosclerotic lesions. Skim milk, instead of being a healthy choice to prevent heart disease, actually puts a substance in your body that causes heart disease. Also, eating a high-protein diet in the absence of fat depletes the body of vitamin A, which can lead to autoimmune diseases, blindness, and cancer.

Most recently, skim milk has been linked to prostate cancer, but whole milk has not. It's very likely that the non-fat dry milk powder and lack of fat are responsible for the connection. It is also interesting to note that farmers feed pigs skim milk to make them fat. Pigs will not get fat on whole milk.

Antibiotics and hormones

Confined cows get sick more often and die earlier than cows allowed the freedom to graze. Antibiotics used to treat sick cows end up in the milk for consumers to eat and may be partly responsible for the increase in antibiotic resistant bacteria. Hormones, which also end up in milk, are given to cows to increase milk production. Recombinant BGH is one such hormone that the FDA allows in milk without it being labeled. Canada has banned the use of rBGH because it increases mastitis in cows leading to increased numbers of white blood cells in the milk along with the antibiotics used to treat the mastitis. Milk from rBGH-treated cows also contains excessive levels of insulin-like growth factor, which may cause cancer.

Ultra-pasteurized milk (UHT)

As if pasteurized milk wasn't bad enough, now we have milk that is heated to extremely high temperatures (280 degrees F) to completely sterilize the milk. This ultra-pasteurized milk can be kept in an aseptic container on a store shelf for six months and in regular containers in the refrigerated section for 50 days. For comparison, raw milk begins to sour between 7 and 10 days.

Ultra-pasteurized milk is so sterile that bugs won't even eat it. We do want foods to spoil in a reasonable time frame because that means that the food contains life-giving properties. Foods that bugs won't eat are completely dead and offer nothing of benefit to the human body. If a bug won't touch it, why would you?

The high temperatures in UHT milk impart a burnt-cabbage-like flavor to the milk that disappears within a few days, but after a month, the milk begins to go "stale," so there is a short window of time when this milk is suitable to drink. But one has to wonder if flavors aren't added to UHT milk to cover the cabbage and stale flavors. If everyone adds flavors, they don't have to be labeled because it's considered an industry standard.

Ultra-pasteurized milk is becoming more popular and may end up as an industry standard. If that happens, UHT milk will no longer need a special label to identify it; the label will simply read "pasteurized" and consumers won't know they are drinking completely dead milk.

Raw milk: it does a body good

Raw milk has nourished humans for thousands of years. J.E. Crewe, MD, a founder of the Mayo Foundation, which was a forerunner to the famous Mayo Clinic, even used raw milk to cure disease. He found that people could get off medications, lose weight, and regain health by consuming nothing but raw milk from grass-fed cows. The treatment was used in many chronic conditions including tuberculosis, diseases of the nervous system, cardiovascular and renal conditions, and hypertension. This treatment protocol, however, was unattractive to physicians and unprofitable for the clinic business. (You mean, all I need is to drink pure grass-fed whole milk?) The milk cure died out because milk can't be patented, it doesn't require a physician or medication, and it uses a relatively inexpensive product. Big business isn't looking for a cheap and easy cure; they want a cure that will put millions, if not billions, of dollars in their pockets.

Raw milk has been described as nature's single most complete food. That is, it has more nutritional essentials in larger amounts than any other food. Milk is good for:

- Reproduction.
- Growth.
- Energy.
- Maintenance and repair.
- Appetite satisfaction.

Raw milk is an outstanding source of calcium and phosphorus for bones and teeth, and contains several B vitamins, including B6, which is only available from raw animal foods. Milk is one of the best sources of B6 since most people do not eat raw meat. Vitamin B12 is another hard-to-come-by vitamin found only in animal foods, and it is necessary for the prevention of pernicious anemia. Whole raw milk also provides significant amounts of vitamins A and D, activator X, and the Wulzen anti-stiffness factor.

All raw-milk dairy foods are healthy, including cheese, yogurt, kefir, cream, sour cream, and butter. Ice cream made from raw cream is much healthier and tastier than store-bought ice cream, but still contains sugar and should be consumed in moderation.

Raw milk is hard to come by in some states, and most states have restrictive laws regarding raw milk, but it is worth the effort to seek it out. Fortunately, there are organizations such as the Weston A. Price Foundation that are working hard to make and keep the sale of raw milk legal. We live in America and should have the right to buy and consume unadulterated food.

We recommend whole raw milk from well-cared-for, grass-fed Jersey and Guernsey cows or goats because it is much healthier than pasteurized milk. If you're not quite ready to go raw, or if you are unable to get raw milk, at least avoid ultra-pasteurized milk. Most half gallon and smaller sized milks are ultra-pasteurized, including organic milks, while most gallon milks are regularly pasteurized. Also, most creams and half-and-halfs are ultra-pasteurized. Choose whole milk over reduced-fat or skim milks, and definitely avoid milk alternatives such as soy and rice milks. Even better, choose cultured dairy products such as full-fat cheese, whole milk yogurt, and kefir.

For more information on raw milk or to find a source, go to www. realmilk.com.

TAKE HOME MESSAGE

1. Drink raw milk if you can.

2. Drink full-fat milk instead of low-fat or skim milk.

3. Avoid ultra-pasteurized milk, soy milk, and rice milk.

4. Eat full-fat yogurt and kefir if you can't get raw milk.

Superfoods

Microwaves and fast food may seem like culinary wonders in our hurried and hectic world, but we've paid a price to have these modern conveniences. As we've abandoned our aprons and chef hats, we've lost the art of preparing deliciously healthy superfoods that boost our immune system, provide energy and prevent disease. If we want to experience real health, we need to get back in the kitchen to rediscover some old, timeless wonders and culinary greats.

Coconut

The coconut is one of the healthiest foods on the planet and is actually used by doctors in tropical locations to improve the health of their patients. Coconut oil is over ninety percent saturated fat and is a solid at room temperature. It is excellent for cooking and frying because it is a highly stable fat that won't go rancid easily. The saturated fats in coconut oil are mostly medium chain triglycerides (MCTs) (perhaps you've heard of MCT oil). MCTs tend to be burned as energy rather than stored in the body. They increase metabolism making it a little easier to lose weight. People with gallbladder disease (a disease that makes it difficult to digest fat) can usually tolerate coconut oil because MCTs don't require bile to be digested and absorbed.

Lauric acid, one of the fatty acids in coconut oil, has antimicrobial properties, which means it can help fight off infections such as sore throats, colds, and food poisoning. Other fatty acids in coconut are used to treat yeast infections. The fatty acids in coconut are highly beneficial to the immune system and provide natural antibiotic protection.

We recommend including coconut in your diet on a daily basis. Coconut oil can be added to yogurt, smoothies, hot tea, and broth. For weight loss, use 2 to 4 Tbsp. of coconut oil daily. It will also help regulate your appetite and give you energy.

Bone broths

Before the invention of skinless chicken breasts, lean steaks, and headless fish, chickens were sold whole and meats came on the bone with fat. In those days, every part of the animal was used. Wonderful broths were made from fish heads and whole chickens (including organs and feet). Broth or stock was the backbone of the diet and used to create marvelous soups and mouth watering sauces.

These rich stocks added flavor to meals and contained several health-enhancing properties. Vinegar was added to broths to draw out minerals from bone such as calcium, magnesium and potassium. Minerals are now severely lacking in our modern diet because we take short cuts in the kitchen and eat foods devoid of nutrients. Broth is a source of gelatin, which is a great digestive aid and very soothing for gastrointestinal problems such as heartburn, Crohn's, ulcerative colitis, and irritable bowel syndrome. Gelatin also enhances our ability to use protein from food for important functions in the body. Another health-enhancing component in broths is cartilage, which has been used in the treatment of cancer and in alleviating painful arthritis and other inflammatory diseases.

Chicken broth has been used for centuries as a cure for colds and flu, while fish stocks have been used to enhance thyroid function and restore energy and vitality. Fish heads contain the thyroid gland and thyroid hormone as well as important minerals such as iodine.

It is well worth the effort to include bone broths in your diet, and it really isn't hard to do. Homemade broths are superior to store bought as they are made with better ingredients and do not contain MSG or other harmful substances. Most soups on the market are highly processed and don't confer any health advantages. The best place to start is on page 124 of *Nourishing Traditions* by Sally Fallon. The chicken broth is fantastic and very simple. Put it on in the evening and let it simmer while you sleep. Strain the broth and use the chicken meat in chicken and rice soup for dinner and make chicken salad for lunch. If you're short on money, broths are a great way to get the nutrition your body craves without the cost of expensive meats.

Organ meats

Once a staple of the diet, organ meats were practically banished from the kitchen in the late 1970s. Organ meats were prized by primitive peoples and provided mothers with an inexpensive way to nourish their children. Even tigers enjoy organ meats, so much so that they eat the organs first. Back in the old days, raw liver was one of baby's first foods. Today kids don't even know what liver or organ meats are.

Organ meats are an excellent source for vitamins A and D as well as essential fatty acids and minerals. In traditional cultures, organ meats were found to provide strength and vitality. The July 1951 issue of *Proceedings for the Society for Experimental Biology and Medicine contained a study on rats consisting of three groups with twelve rats in each group.* The first group ate a basic diet fortified with eleven vitamins. The second group ate the same diet along with an additional supply of vitamin B complex. The third group ate the original diet, but instead of vitamin B complex, received ten percent of rations as powdered liver.

A 1975 article published in *Prevention* magazine described the experiment as follows: "After several weeks, the animals were placed one by one into a drum of cold water from which they could not climb out. They literally were forced to sink or swim. Rats in the first group swam for an average of 13.3 minutes before giving up. The second group, which had the added fortifications of

B vitamins, swam for an average of 13.4 minutes. Of the last group of rats, the ones receiving liver, three swam for 63, 83 and 87 minutes. The other nine rats in this group were still swimming vigorously at the end of two hours when the test was terminated. Something in the liver had prevented them from becoming exhausted. To this day scientists have not been able to pin a label on this anti-fatigue factor."

If organ meats are so good for us, why don't we eat them anymore? When cholesterol became a dreaded villain, liver was accused of being dangerous for the heart since it contained a high amount of cholesterol. Even though liver and other organ meats kept traditional cultures healthy to a ripe old age, it would now send us to an early grave. The traditional cultures didn't know about the alleged dangers of cholesterol, so the health authorities probably applied the old saying, "What you don't know can't hurt you." So far, there is no evidence to support cholesterol's bad rap.

Liver is also high in vitamin A, and most health authorities believe the vitamin to be toxic. Real vitamin A is not toxic, but synthetic vitamin A is. Toxins are sent to the liver for detoxification, so it is assumed that if you eat liver, you are also eating whatever toxins the animal ate. Toxins are not stored in the liver; they are processed there and then sent on their way. However, if a liver is overloaded with toxins, it may not be able to process them and some of those toxins will remain in the liver. This is the only reason to avoid organ meats that has any validity, but it is easily overcome by purchasing organic liver from grass-fed animals. Also, the nutritional benefits of the liver far outweigh any toxins you might consume and your liver would be able to eliminate any toxins coming in, especially if you are following the principles of the Liberation Diet.

The bottom line is there is no good reason to avoid organ meats. Liver used to be consumed once a week, and we need to get back to that. It's okay to start slow. Shred liver and add it to ground meat to use in burgers, tacos or casseroles; you won't even know it's there. Use other organ meats the same way, and remember to add organ meats to stocks to boost the nutrient content.

Fermented foods

Before the invention of the ice box, traditional cultures had to find ways to preserve food so that during times of plenty, some of the food could be preserved to use for times of famine. They discovered fermentation, a method of preservation where yeast and bacteria convert carbohydrates into alcohol, lactic acid, or acetic acid. In addition to preserving food, fermentation has other benefits including:

- Enhancement of enzyme content.
- Aiding digestion.
- Synthesis of important nutrients.
- Elimination of anti-nutrients.
- Reducing carbohydrate content.
- Improvement in flavor and aroma.

Almost everything that goes on in the human body requires enzymes. We need enzymes to digest food, convert fat and glucose to energy, make hormones, and more. The body makes most of the enzymes needed for digestion, but some food substances require enzymes that humans don't have. For instance, legumes contain two sugars that humans cannot break down because we lack the necessary enzyme. If we soak the beans for a long period of time with a little acid, enzyme inhibitors are neutralized and the difficult-to-digest sugars are broken down before we eat them. Not only can fermentation provide enzymes we don't have, it can also spare the enzyme stores we do have. Food enzymes "predigest" food, making it much easier and less stressful for the body to assimilate nutrients from foods.

Fermented foods are a great digestive aid, and you only need small amounts with each meal. Before modern processing, condiments such as ketchup, mustard, and relish were fermented and added to meals in small quantities to help digest the meal. Fermented foods are wonderful soothers and healing superfoods for people suffering from gastrointestinal problems from heartburn to ulcerative colitis, because the bacteria from these fermented foods enhance the growth of intestinal flora, the good bacteria in the gut. These good bacteria help prevent food-borne illness caused by E. coli and salmonella. Junk foods, antibiotics, pollution, stress, and refined carbohydrates make our digestive system weak and promote the overgrowth of E. coli in the gut, which can lead to all manner of health problems. Fermented foods can restore your health and increase your lifespan.

Bacteria, during the fermenting process, can actually synthesize B vitamins and vitamin C, so fermented foods have increased amounts of important health-building nutrients. Soaking flour in buttermilk or yogurt, or whole grains in water with a couple tablespoons of acid (lemon juice, vinegar or whey) for twelve to twenty-four hours will make the final product more nutritious and more digestible. For quick breads, flour is soaked in an equal amount of yogurt or buttermilk and left out, covered with a cloth, for at least twelve hours. The remaining ingredients are added after soaking, but the leavening agent and amount may need to change. Usually, one teaspoon of baking soda is used for each cup of flour. Unfortunately, this process doesn't work well for cookies or cakes. Fermenting also neutralizes anti-nutrients such as phytic acid, which binds to calcium, magnesium, zinc, and other minerals taking them out of the body before we have a chance to use them. Fermenting adds nutrients and makes the already present nutrients available for the body to use, creating a truly superfood without harmful additives.

We have great news for you carb lovers. During the fermentation process, bacteria convert sugar and starch into lactic acid and carbon dioxide, magically transforming high-carb foods into low-carb extreme superfoods! Now you can have your bread and eat it, too.

Along with all the marvelous health benefits of fermented foods comes improvement in flavor and aroma. Compare cabbage to sauerkraut or cucumbers to pickles. You get a nice tang with the sauerkraut and pickles and a much better aroma. The best part of fermentation is that it is really easy to do. Get the *Nourishing Traditions* cookbook and start with the salsa recipe on page 103, as Americans are not accustomed to the improved flavor of fermented foods. Salsa ferments nicely and will help train your taste buds for other flavors.

One last thing about fermentation; soy absolutely must be fermented for at least six months in order to be edible because it contains a plethora of anti-nutrients and enzyme inhibitors that can destroy your health. Fermented soy includes naturally fermented soy sauce (not Kikoman), miso, tempeh and natto. The processed and unfermented soy products on supermarket shelves such as soy milk, soy flour, soy protein isolate, soy nuts, and edamame should be avoided. Contrary to popular belief, processed soy is not a health food and most soy consumed in Asian countries is fermented. Unfermented soy can lead to infertility and hypothyroidism and is especially dangerous for children.

Cultured dairy

Cultured dairy foods such as yogurt, crème fraiche, cream cheese, piima cream, cheese, and kefir are produced when bacteria digest milk sugar (lactose) and milk protein (casein), forming lactic acid. When enough lactic acid has been produced to inactivate all the putrefying bacteria, the cultured product will last several weeks. Cheese undergoes additional fermentation and can last for years.

People with milk allergies can often tolerate yogurt and kefir because the offending components in milk, the lactose and casein, have been digested for them by the bacteria. Enzymes destroyed in pasteurized milk are restored in cultured dairy foods and the vitamin B and C content of the milk is increased. Cultured milk products also send beneficial bacteria and lactic acid to the digestive tract, aiding digestion and preventing harmful pathogens from causing illness. Yogurt and kefir are wonderful additions to the diet, providing a tolerable source of calcium and many immune enhancing qualities.

Probiotics are the latest fashion in supplements, but why take a pill when you could have some good old-fashioned yogurt or a tasty dill? Cultured dairy and fermented foods are the best source of probiotics, and they come with important nutrients and life-giving enzymes. Just make sure your dairy is full-fat.

TAKE HOME MESSAGE

1. Eat chicken broth, organ meats, yogurt, and kefir.

2. Prepare grains properly by soaking, sprouting or sour leavening.

3. Get the cookbook *Nourishing Traditions* by Sally Fallon.

Supplements

You want to be healthy and take all the right supplements, but how do you know what you really need? Health food stores and supermarket shelves are cluttered with all kinds of pills, potions, and powders, all promising longevity and good health, creating a confusing maze that never ends. We all have different needs for different nutrients, but there are a few supplements that benefit everyone.

Diet comes first

First, we need to put supplements in their place. You can't fix a bad diet by popping pills. Supplements do not make up for a diet devoid of nutrients; they add to or enhance a diet of whole, unprocessed foods. The diet is the first line of defense against disease and obesity.

When it comes to nutrition, what matters most is what is actually absorbed and utilized by the body. Food contains nutrients in the proper balance so that deficiencies do not occur. Supplements on the other hand, may contain too much of one mineral or vitamin and not enough of another. Many vitamins and minerals compete with each other for absorption, so the right balance is critical to get everything you need. Taking high doses of single nutrients can leave you deficient in some other critical nutrient. Whole foods also contain co-factors, enzymes, and other components that aid in the digestion and absorption of nutrients. The science of nutrition is still relatively new, so some of the beneficial substances in food haven't even been discovered yet.

Now that you have the right perspective, following are the supplements we recommend.

Cod liver oil

Cod liver oil is one of the best natural sources of vitamins A and D. It also provides the healthy omega-3 fatty acids found in regular fish oil. There are two different kinds of cod liver oil: regular and high vitamin. We recommend the high-vitamin cod liver oil from Green Pastures because it has a better ratio of vitamins A and D. If you also want a good source of activator X, or vitamin K2, without taking a second pill, we recommend Green Pastures Blue Ice Gold Therapeutics. This product contains both high-vitamin cod liver oil and high-vitamin butter oil, which provides a wonderful mix of healthy fatty acids, vitamins A, D and K2. Dr. Price noted that cod liver oil was much more effective when taken with high-vitamin butter oil. You can find this product at www.visionarytrainers.com.

Essential minerals

Over ninety percent of our bodily functions work in the presence of minerals. Most people take calcium supplements and some may take a magnesium supplement or zinc when they feel a cold coming on, but few people recognize their need for trace minerals. Trace minerals are required by the body in very small amounts, but without them, we can't function properly. The mineral content of foods varies because it is dependent on the level of minerals in the soil and on the amount of processing to which the food was subjected. Deficient soil produces plants with lower levels of minerals, and processing strips most minerals from the food. On the Liberation Diet, you won't be eating many processed foods, but it's not likely you'll be able to check the soil content of all your food. We recommend New Vision Essential Minerals. It comes from organic plant sources and contains over seventy major and trace minerals in a liquid form for better absorption. You can find this product at www.visionarytrainers.com.

Mangosteen juice

We live in a very toxic world, with pollution, harmful plastics, stress, and contaminated water forcing our bodies to work hard to remove toxins before they can cause health problems. Antioxidants are one of the body's defense mechanisms, and we need to consume more of them. Antioxidants protect the body against free radicals, helping the body prevent diseases such as cancer and heart disease. The mangosteen fruit, grown mostly in Thailand, contains a variety of super antioxidants known as xanthones. Xanthones have a wide array of beneficial effects on the body due to their anti-bacterial, anti-viral, anti-fungal, and anti-tumor properties. The mangosteen is one of the healthiest foods on the planet, and we recommend it as a supplement in whole food form. For more information and to order the brand we recommend, go to www.visionarytrainers.discovermangosteen.com.

Whole body multiples

For those of you who want some extra insurance or need a little extra nutrition due to a disease process or family history of chronic disease, Annette has formulated a high quality multiple vitamin with highly bio-available forms of nutrients from natural sources. This unique multiple contains nutrients that help with blood sugar and homocysteine (a marker for heart disease) control as well as nutrients that fight free radicals, improve cellular energy, and promote detoxification. You can find more information at www.findyourweigh.com.

Start with the basics

For most people, the above supplements added to the Liberation Diet principles will be all you need to enjoy good health. If you have an existing health condition, family history of chronic disease, or take medication, you may benefit from additional supplements. For more information or help in designing an individualized diet and supplement plan, go to www.visionarytrainers.com or www.findyourweigh. com.

TAKE HOME MESSAGE

1. The diet is most important.

2. Supplements do not make up for a bad diet.

3. Whole food supplements are the best.

Putting It All Together

By now you have an idea of what you shouldn't be eating and are probably wondering if there is anything you can eat. We have good news. The Liberation Diet consists of foods that are not only healthy, but incredibly tasty, too. Real food contains flavors that fake food can't mimic, but some of you may need time to adjust to those flavors. We know people who actually prefer the taste of margarine to butter simply because that is what they grew up eating, so if you need to mix fake food with real food until you develop a taste for real food, you can. For example, mix ¾ cup margarine with ¼ cup butter until you get used to the taste. Then use ½ cup margarine and ½ cup butter followed by ¼ cup margarine and ¾ cup butter. Next, leave out the margarine. You have essentially weaned yourself off margarine and are now able to enjoy real butter. If you are drinking skim milk, use the same formula to gradually switch to whole milk.

Following are the basic principles of the Liberation Diet.

Fats

Fat is the most important nutrient in the diet and should comprise at least fifty percent of your diet. Half of your fat intake should be from saturated fats found in animal foods, coconut, and palm oils. About five percent of your fat intake should consist of polyunsaturated fats, which include the all important omega-3 fats. Polyunsaturated fats are found in nuts, seeds, nut and seed oils, and fish. The remainder of your fat intake will consist of monounsaturated fats such as those in olive oil and avocados. All fats contain a mixture of saturated, polyunsaturated, and monounsaturated fats, so if you eat whole foods, you will get the right balance. We recommend using extra virgin coconut and olive oils, and any other oils such as sesame and sunflower should be unrefined. Lard should not contain hydrogenated fat.

Saturated fats are best for high temperature cooking/frying as they are the most stable and less likely to go rancid. Olive oil can be used for sautéing. Never reuse cooking oil. Avoid soybean, corn, cottonseed, and canola oils and any oils that have been hydrogenated or interesterified. And don't forget to use coconut oil every day.

ON THE LIBERATION DIET

USE THIS...	INSTEAD OF THIS...
Coconut oil, butter, lard, palm oil	Shortening, margarine
Equal parts coconut oil, olive oil, sesame oil	Vegetable oil, canola oil
Beef tallow, lard	Hydrogenated oils, soybean oil
Full-fat sour cream	Fat-free or reduced-fat sour cream
Whole milk	Skim or low-fat milk
Whole fat yogurt/cottage cheese	Fat-free or low-fat yogurt/cottage cheese
Safflower oil mayonnaise	Soybean/canola oil mayonnaise
Real whipped cream	Cool whip
Full-fat salad dressing	Fat-free or reduced-fat salad dressing
Full-fat cheese	Fat-free, reduced-fat or processed cheese

A word of caution about fat: If you have been following a low-fat diet, you may need to gradually increase your fat intake so your gallbladder can adjust. Otherwise you might experience diarrhea or stomach ache. Increase fat by five grams per day. If you feel nauseous, cut back, and increase at a slower rate.

Proteins

Any protein that comes from an animal is recommended on the Liberation Diet, such as egg, beef, lamb, turkey, chicken, duck, goose, fish, lobster, crab, shrimp, fish, roe, milk, yogurt, cheese, venison, and buffalo. Grass-fed beef and cage-free poultry are preferred over beef and chicken that have been fed grains and soy. Also, meats should not contain antibiotics or hormones. You want full-fat hamburger and meats that have not been trimmed of fat if possible. Don't buy skin-less chicken. The skin is incredibly healthy and very tasty.

Soy and other plant proteins are not recommended as they do not contain the right balance of amino acids. They also do not contain adequate amounts of fat, which is necessary for the proper digestion and absorption of protein. Animal protein has superior vitamin and mineral content as well. Humans are omnivores. We are designed to eat both animal and plant foods, but our digestive tracts are better suited to digest animal protein than plant protein.

Nuts in small amounts provide protein and minerals, but nuts should be soaked in salt water and then dehydrated to remove anti-nutrients. The best nuts are almonds and walnuts.

Organ meats

Organ meats such as liver, kidney, tripe, and heart supply fat soluble vitamins and are supremely nutritious. Include organ meats in your diet at least once a week. You can hide them in ground meat if necessary. It is best to use organ meats from grass-fed animals as they will contain fewer toxins.

Bone-broth soup

Broth, whether it's chicken, beef, duck, or fish, should be made weekly and used for making soups, sauces, and gravies. Broth can also be used as a beverage with a meal. Homemade broths provide hard-to-get minerals.

Fermented foods

Fermented foods are recommended at every meal as an aid to digestion. Making them is fun and fairly easy, but you may also be able to find some in health food stores. Sauerkraut, kefir, yogurt, and beet kvass are just a few examples of fermented foods.

Vegetables

Properly prepared vegetables are certainly healthy, but vegetables are not the foundation of health. They should be eaten in smaller proportion to the fat and protein. All vegetables can be eaten on the Liberation Diet, but the starchy vegetables like corn, peas, and potatoes should be eaten sparingly. Serve vegetables with butter and a little sea salt. You always want to eat vegetables with fat, preferably saturated fat, to increase the absorption of antioxidants, vitamins, and minerals. Raw broccoli, cauliflower, cabbage, and Brussels sprouts should be avoided or eaten infrequently as they contain a substance that interferes with thyroid function; they are best eaten cooked. Spinach is best cooked as well to neutralize oxalic acid, an anti-nutrient that binds to calcium and takes it out of the body. Vegetables are best if locally grown without pesticides and in season. Take advantage of any farmer's markets near you.

Fruits

Fruits should be eaten even less frequently than vegetables and should only be eaten when in season. The riper a fruit is, the more sugar it contains. High-sugar fruits like bananas are best eaten a little on the green side. The best fruits are berries, as they are lower in carbohydrate content and high in antioxidants. Fruit is best eaten with real cream or some other healthy fat to increase absorption of antioxidants. Organic, locally grown fruits are recommended, especially for strawberries, apples, pears and grapes, and we recommend limiting fruits to no more than two servings per day. You may even want to go lower while losing weight.

Grains and legumes

Grains and legumes are high carbohydrate foods. They also contain anti-nutrients and need to be properly prepared by soaking or sprouting. It is best to avoid grains and legumes while you are losing weight. Once the weight is off, you can include up to two servings per day. Organic grains and legumes are recommended. Homemade popcorn with real butter or coconut oil can be enjoyed on occasion. Skip the microwave popcorn entirely.

Beverages

Americans drink entirely too much, whether it's water, juice, soda or coffee. As a general rule, let thirst be your guide to how much you need to drink. It is best not to drink within an hour of eating, but if you need a liquid at meals, try milk, broth, or a fermented drink.

Diet soda is a poison, so we don't recommend it at all (see Artificial Sweeteners below). Regular soda isn't much better, so we recommend avoiding soda entirely, or at least limiting soda to no more than one 12-oz. can per week. Sodas with natural sugars are better than sodas with high fructose corn syrup, but homemade lacto-fermented sodas are even better.

Caffeine will give you an energy boost, but it will generally be followed by a crash in energy. The adrenal glands that control hormone balance can be over-stimulated by caffeine, so we recommend avoiding caffeinated beverages such as coffee and tea. But we realize some of you are going to insist on your cup of Joe, so at least limit the coffee to one or two cups per day. If you are tired all the time, it would be best to avoid caffeinated coffee entirely. Energy drinks are usually loaded with caffeine and sugar, so avoid them completely. You don't need that kind of energy.

Alcohol should be avoided or limited to a daily glass of red wine while losing weight. Even though some beer and wine have some redeeming nutritional properties, alcohol can interfere with absorption of vitamins and cause you to put on extra weight. Once you've lost your weight and if you must drink, keep it below two drinks per day and make sure you eat some fat. Fat protects the liver from the toxic effects of alcohol.

Following is a list of acceptable beverages. We recommend them unsweetened or with a little stevia (a very sweet herb):

- Raw milk
- Kefir
- Lacto-fermented beverages and soda
- Iced tea
- Green tea
- Herbal tea
- Yerba mate
- Xango and water or water and minerals (homemade sports drink)
- Fresh juice mixed with water (use sparingly)

Sweet treats

While it would be best for our bodies to avoid sweets entirely, a little chocolate makes life more pleasant and, realistically, we aren't going to cut sweets out of the diet. We need to find a good balance. The best sugars are rapadura (unprocessed cane sugar), molasses, pure maple syrup, and raw honey. Stevia and laktano are acceptable low-calorie sweeteners. Here are a few tips for including sweets in a healthy diet:

- **Follow the 80/20 rule.** If you eat healthy foods eighty percent of the time, you can eat not-so-healthy foods twenty percent of the time. With this rule, you don't have to worry about birthdays and anniversaries. Just enjoy.

- **Every meal does not require a dessert.** Dessert accompanies everything from coffee to steak, but we don't need a constant supply of sweets. Limit high-sugar sweets to one per week and natural treats to one per day.

- **Watch the serving size.** You don't need to eat a whole triple-decker, fudge-filled, ice cream on top, chocolate monster cake. A few bites will do.

- **Make a healthier treat.** Sugar isn't always necessary for a satisfying dessert. Berries topped with real whipped cream is a decadent treat that is also healthy. When making your own treats, use unprocessed cane sugar (rapadura), honey, molasses or maple syrup. You can also cut out at least ¼ cup of sugar in any recipe. Use healthy fats instead of shortening. Coconut flakes mixed with butter makes a delicious pie crust that is healthier than regular crust. Adding vanilla extract and cinnamon can make a treat seem sweeter while using less sugar.

- **Limit sugar alcohols.** Excessive amounts of sugar alcohols can cause gastrointestinal problems, and they are being put into more and more products. Sugar alcohols include mannitol, xylitol, malitol, and sorbitol.

- **Use natural low-calorie sugars if desired.** Currently, there are two good options for low calorie sweeteners: stevia and laktano. Stevia is an herb that is incredibly sweet. It comes in powder or liquid and even in flavors. Laktano is a combination of fermented erythritol (a sugar alcohol) and luo han guo (a Chinese plant) and has been used in Japan for nearly a decade. Laktano can be used in place of an equal amount of sugar and can be heated. The drawback to laktano is that it has an alcohol sort of after-feel in the mouth, and it is quite expensive. These low-calorie sugars are not necessary as you won't be eating many sweets anyway. The best way to use low-calorie sweeteners is in drinks and salad dressings—foods that need small amounts of sugar.

Your desire for sweets will diminish once you get going on the Liberation Diet because your body will overcome its addiction to sugar. You will also be getting all the nutrients you need, so you will not have cravings anymore.

Artificial sweeteners

Obesity rates have increased since the invention of artificial sweeteners, so they obviously do nothing to help you maintain a normal weight. Many of them have not been tested adequately and some of the most popular sweeteners cause serious side effects. Aspartame (Equal), sucralose (Splenda), saccharin (Sweet'n Low), neotame and acesulfame-K are artificial sweeteners that should be avoided, with Aspartame being the worst offender.

Aspartame is a poison and a neurotoxin that can lead to Parkinson's or Alzheimer's later in life and may cause autoimmune disorders such as fibromyalgia and multiple sclerosis. It also blocks the production of serotonin, a brain chemical that helps regulate appetite. Low serotonin levels cause you to crave carbohydrates, and as we've shown earlier in the book, carbohydrates cause you to store fat due to its effect on insulin.

One of the components of Aspartame is methanol, which breaks down to formate that will either be excreted or converted to formaldehyde. Two recent studies that show the dangers of aspartame can be found in the *European Journal of Clinical Nutrition*, 2007 Aug 8 (The direct and indirect cellular effects of aspartame on the brain), and in *Environmental Health Perspective*, 2007 Sept.; 115(9):1293–7 (Life span exposure to low doses of aspartame beginning during prenatal life increases cancer effects in rats).

Give thanks

One of the most overlooked parts of a meal is giving thanks. When we eat, it is an opportunity to remember the many blessings our Creator gives to us and how faithful He is to feed us each and every day. Giving thanks has been a tradition among Americans since the pilgrims landed at Plymouth Rock but has recently gone out of style, especially as snacking and eating on the run replace the family meal. We believe prayer needs to be brought back to the dinner table. It is difficult to eat like a glutton when you invite God into the meal. When we eat with thanksgiving, it changes our attitude about food and helps us gain control over addictions and overeating. When we take prayer out, it opens the door for the random eating of fake food and sweets that has led to the obesity epidemic we face now. Giving thanks gives us cause to reflect and ask ourselves, "Do I really need to eat this microwave popcorn or ice cream float?" Being thankful changes the way we think and focuses our minds on the positive instead of the negative, improving our health and wellbeing. Giving thanks shouldn't be limited to one day of the year. It is designed to be given before every meal.

Slow down

Most of us rush from one event to another, and we even rush through our meals. If we want to be healthy, we need to slow down and take our meals one bite at a time. Your body has a chew clock that signals the brain when your body is full of nutrients. If you eat too quickly, you will often eat more than you need before your brain gets the memo. Digestion begins in the mouth, and the more you chew your food, the more digestible it becomes and the easier it is for your digestive system to process the food. So take the time to chew and have some conversation while you're eating to help slow down the movement of the fork from plate to mouth.

Meal frequency

We recommend eating two or three meals a day. If you are eating enough fat, you shouldn't get hungry between meals. Snacking is discouraged, but if you must snack, pick foods that are high in protein and fat and avoid high-carbohydrate foods.

Breakfast

If you choose to eat breakfast, we highly recommend eggs. Farm fresh eggs from free range hens are best followed by organic omega-3 rich eggs at the supermarket. Cheap supermarket eggs contain lower amounts of fat-soluble vitamins and minerals than farm fresh eggs because the hens live in confinement and do not get much sun. Eggs can be accompanied by bacon, sausage, ham, fish, scrapple, or raw milk if desired. Eggs can be scrambled, fried, poached or put into omelets. Use coconut oil or butter for the frying.

If you can't live without cereal, we recommend steel cut oats, properly soaked and served with butter or coconut oil. Avoid cold, processed, and instant cereals. Pancakes and waffles that have been properly prepared are acceptable with lots of butter and a little pure maple syrup. These breakfast foods should be accompanied by some protein such as eggs, meats, or milk.

A great accompaniment to any breakfast is a half cup of warm chicken broth with coconut oil.

Lunch and dinner

Both lunch and dinner meals are similar in their structure. You may have any protein you like, such as beef, fish, chicken, shrimp, lamb, lobster, turkey, veal, duck, meatloaf, pork, and sausage. Eggs are also great for lunch and dinner, even if you had them for breakfast. You can have as many eggs as you want on the Liberation Diet. Be sure to cook your proteins with some healthy fat such as lard, coconut oil, butter, or palm oil. Having fat and protein at every meal is critical for good health!

In addition to protein and fat, add some vegetables with butter. Salads with meat and homemade dressing make a great meal with some yogurt and berries. Cream cheese and avocado can be wrapped up in deli meats for a great portable lunch. Serve with veggie sticks with sour-cream-based dip and a cup of kefir for a filling meal. Soups and stews make great cold weather meals.

Eating out

If you only eat out once a week or less, you don't have to worry too much about your menu choices, but if you eat out a lot, you need to be extra cautious. Most restaurants use MSG in their foods, so the first thing you want to do is ask what menu items do not contain MSG. Generally, getting foods prepared without sauces and seasonings is a good way to avoid MSG.

Choose meats and non-starchy vegetables. Avoid potatoes, beans, and rice, and ask the server not to bring bread and chips to the table. If you must have the bread, limit it to one slice, roll, or stick, and put butter on it. Put avocados, nuts, and cheese on salads, and use olive oil and vinegar dressing or bring your own. Most salad dressings contain unhealthy oils, but you can always ask the server what type of oil is used.

Most restaurants serve mammoth portions, so split a meal with someone else or box up half of it before you start eating. This will help control portion size. Eat slowly and skip the soda and French fries.

Avoid buffets if you can, but if you must go, fill your plate once and don't go back for seconds. You don't need to get your money's worth because it will just end up on your hips, which will mean spending extra money to get it off your hips. When you fill your plate, don't allow the different foods to touch. This will automatically control the amount of food you can put on a plate.

Eating at someone else's house

You will most likely end up with friends and family who don't agree with the Liberation Diet principles, and you may find yourself at their house to eat. Don't worry, just eat whatever they serve. You can take smaller portions of grains and larger portions of meats. You can also volunteer to bring a dish.

Supplements

We recommend taking cod liver oil in the morning with mangosteen juice before breakfast. If you are taking a multivitamin, take half in the morning and half in the evening.

Label reading

Food labels are, for the most part, a waste of time because they don't tell you much. Following are a few guidelines to choosing packaged foods:

- Ignore health claims on the packaging.

- **Read the ingredient list first.** Put the item back on the shelf if it contains hydrogenated or interesterified oils, high fructose corn syrup, aspartame, or MSG.

- **Look at the carbohydrate and sugar content.** Put the item back on the shelf if it contains more than 12 grams of carbohydrate or 5 grams of sugar.

- **Look at the sodium content.** If it contains more than 200 mg of sodium, put it back on the shelf.

That's all you need to pay attention to. The vitamin content is not accurate and doesn't apply to individuals, so ignore all the "percent daily value" stuff. Calories don't matter on the Liberation Diet because you won't be eating a lot of carbohydrate foods.

A word on food combining

The theory of food combining emerged in the early 1900s before we understood how the digestive system worked. This theory basically restricts putting alkaline foods with acid foods. Proteins can't be eaten with starch, fruit, or fat, and fruit must be eaten alone. The only food group that combines with anything, except fruit, is vegetables. The claim is that proper food combining improves digestion and prevents food from putrefying in the stomach, but there is no scientific support for this type of food combining. The only purpose it serves is to make meal planning incredibly complicated.

Most foods are a combination of starch, protein, and fat. If starch cannot be eaten with protein, we could not eat grains or legumes since they contain significant amounts of starch and protein. Nuts and whole fat dairy foods would be off the menu since they contain both fat and protein. Regardless of what you eat, the stomach is very acidic and the intestines are very alkaline. God designed the digestive tract in such a way that you can digest carbohydrate, fat, and protein at the same time. Digestion of starch begins in the mouth, stops in the stomach, and resumes again in the intestine. Protein and fat digestion begins in the stomach and continues in the intestines. The majority of digestion and absorption occurs in the small intestines. While fat does keep food in the stomach longer, that food does not stay there long enough to putrefy. The benefit of food staying longer in the stomach and intestines is that more nutrients are absorbed by the body.

There are some food combining techniques that are simple and effective, however. Combining anything with fat increases the absorption of vitamins, minerals, and antioxidants and also lowers the glycemic index of the food. Combining lacto-fermented foods with any other food improves digestion and spares body enzymes. We do not advocate a vegetarian diet, but for those who want to remain vegetarian, combining grains with legumes or nuts enhances the amino acid profile, providing a more complete protein (of course, those grains, legumes, and nuts need to be prepared properly). Combining dairy foods or eggs with vegetarian diets also greatly improves the nutritional quality of the diet.

We believe there are more important things to do in life than micromanaging your diet. Eating should be natural and easy to figure out. If you eat real food the way God made it, your digestive tract will take good care of you.

Getting Started

The Liberation Diet is a lifestyle diet, meaning it is not a diet you go on to lose weight and go off when you've lost the weight. Most people will need to make significant changes in what and how they eat, so we don't expect you to go cold turkey. The goal is not to get on the diet as fast as you can, but to maintain the lifestyle once you are on it. Following are steps and principles that will get you started on your journey towards liberating health.

Set a real goal

Before you embark on this journey, you need to know where you want to go, so the first thing you need to do is write down your health goals. Goals need to be SMART: Specific, Measurable, Achievable, Realistic, and they must have a Timeframe. A goal is only a dream if it doesn't have a date attached to it.

"I would like to lose twenty pounds," for example, sounds more like a pipedream than a serious goal. But, "I choose to lose twenty pounds by May 15," or "I choose to fit in a size 6 dress for my class reunion May 15," are goals that can be measured and they have a timeframe to keep you focused. You don't need an excuse such as a class reunion to lose weight and get healthy, but it can help motivate you.

How do you know if your goals are achievable and realistic? If today is January 1 and you are 100 pounds overweight, an unrealistic goal would be, "I choose to lose seventy-five pounds by February 1." You may have a timeframe, but one month isn't enough time to lose seventy-five pounds. We recommend setting goals to lose ten pounds at a time, and definitely no more than twenty. When you achieve that goal, set another ten-pound goal and keep going until all your weight is lost. At the end of each ten pounds, reward yourself.

You can reasonably lose one to two pounds per week. On the Liberation Diet, most people lose more than that, particularly at first, but the one to two pounds is a reasonable goal. If you lose more than two pounds per week, you just complete your goal before the deadline and there isn't anything wrong with that. It's a much better position to be in than not completing your goal on time. If you need to lose 100 lbs and today is January 1, count ahead five weeks to February 5. In five weeks, you should be able to lose five to ten lbs. Your goal may be, "I choose to lose ten pounds by February 5." When that goal is achieved, reward yourself with a new outfit, exercise equipment, painting, kitchen gadget, spa treatment, or anything else that does not involve food. Pat yourself on the back and write another goal. If you only lose seven pounds in five weeks, reward yourself, pat yourself on the back, and write a new goal. Losing seven pounds instead of ten is still moving in the right direction.

If you can't measure it, you can't manage it. So we recommend a digital scale that can be purchased for a reasonable price at most major retailers like Target or Wal-Mart. Weigh yourself in the morning after you go to the bathroom and before you eat breakfast. Weight fluctuates normally throughout the day and after exercise, so weighing first thing in the morning will give you a more accurate weight. Weigh at least once a week. If you are doing the program correctly, you should be losing weight on a weekly basis. The average weight loss is two pounds per week, but you are still doing great if you only lose one pound or even half a pound per week.

If you haven't lost any weight for two consecutive weeks, it is time to evaluate what you are eating to see if it lines up with the program and make any needed adjustments. If everything seems to be in order with the diet, you may want to check thyroid function and hormone levels. If your hormones are out of whack, it can prevent you from losing weight even if you are eating right. Allergies, medications, and toxic metal buildup are other things that can prevent you from losing weight.

Goals can involve other things besides weight. You may want to fit into a particular dress size or you may want a certain waist measurement. Maybe you want to get off a medication or reduce the amount of medicine you take. Perhaps you want to be able to run a marathon or walk up a flight of steps without wheezing. Whatever you want out of life is the goal. The Liberation Diet is the tool to help you achieve that goal.

Clean out the kitchen

Now that you know where you are going, you need to get rid of things that will prevent you from achieving your goals. Start in the pantry. Eat (if you just can't bear to waste food) or throw out any foods with hydrogenated or interesterified oils; soybean oil, cottonseed, canola, and corn oils; high fructose corn syrup; MSG (including unlabeled MSG); aspartame and other artificial sweeteners; and processed soy. You will also want to toss any bleached flour, refined sugar, shortening, hydrogenated lard, baking powder with aluminum, refined salt, and any spices containing refined salt. Dry cereal, chips, cookies, and crackers need to go.

In the fridge, get rid of unfermented soy foods; condiments with the above ingredients; margarine; fat free or low-fat dressings; imitation syrup; processed cheese; skim or low-fat dairy foods; luncheon meats, bacon, sausage and hot dogs containing nitrates or nitrites; soda and juice.

From the freezer, get rid of any processed meats, refined sweets, frozen veggies with sauces or additives, frozen fruit with sugar, and frozen dinners.

Cleaning out the kitchen can be a tough job, so if you are feeling a little overwhelmed, start with the freezer. Get comfortable with the changes you made in the freezer before moving on to the fridge. When you are comfortable with the changes in the fridge, tackle the pantry. Keep in mind that it isn't a race to see who gets there first. We want you to be able to stay there once you get there.

If you haven't already, pick up some basic cookbooks. First on the list is *Nourishing Traditions* by Sally Fallon and *The Liberation Diet Cookbook* (coming soon). A general cookbook, such as the Better Homes and Gardens version, is good to have as well. Recipes can always be adapted to fit the Liberation Diet principles.

Stock the kitchen

The fake food is gone, so now you need to put in the right foods. In the pantry, you will want sea salt, aluminum-free baking powder, baking soda, rapadura sugar, honey, molasses, coconut milk, unsweetened coconut, extra virgin coconut oil, extra virgin olive oil, raw apple cider vinegar, any other vinegar you like, organic tomato paste/sauce, organic popping corn and carob powder. The spices we use most are pure vanilla extract, garlic powder, onion powder, ginger, turmeric and cinnamon, but any spices you like are fine as long as they don't contain refined salt or MSG. Canned broth such as Health Valley or Shelton's is good to have on hand for emergencies. Just make sure any canned broths or soups are free of MSG and soy ingredients. Jennie's macaroons are an acceptable sweet treat that satisfies without breaking the scale. Garlic, onions, tomatoes, lemons, bananas, and avocados should be kept in dry storage, not the refrigerator.

The fridge should have mayonnaise with safflower oil or any oil besides soybean and canola; organic ketchup and mustard; full-fat sour cream with no additives (Daisy is an excellent brand); full-fat yogurt, milk, kefir, and cheese; fresh vegetables and fruits; butter; unrefined non-toasted sesame oil (toasted sesame oil is also good to have on hand) and unrefined flaxseed oil; eggs; lacto-fermented foods; Eden or San J tamari/soy sauce, pure maple syrup; unbleached white flour, whole grain spelt flour and rye flour; and nuts and whole grains.

The freezer can store meats (preferably grass fed, but at least with no hormones or antibiotics), frozen veggies, and unsweetened fruits, properly prepared breads, whole grains, and real ice cream.

Start locating real food, organic when possible, and begin to stock your house with whole foods. It does take some time to turn over the food supply in the house, but it is fun and a whole new adventure unfolds as you begin to learn about real foods and how to prepare them.

Plan your meals

We live in a busy and hectic world, and everyone wants a piece of us. The kids have music lessons, dance recitals, and soccer games. Parents work hard eight or more hours a day to come home to a messy house, laundry, and hungry kids. Add church activities, volunteer work, and friends and when all is said and done, it's too late to make dinner, so it's off to the nearest drive-through.

Most people fail at the dinner table because they don't take the time to plan. They just bounce from one activity to another hoping that somewhere along the way the body gets the nutrients it needs to stay healthy. But health doesn't happen by accident; you have to plan for it. If it makes you feel better, the authors can't even eat right without a plan and we're nutrition experts.

The first step in meal planning is to decide how slow or how fast you want to get started on a healthy eating plan. For instance, do you want to start planning two meals a week to get the hang of it, or do you want to go full speed ahead and plan out the entire week? Do you want to get the hang of breakfast before you tackle dinner planning? It doesn't really matter what you choose to do as long as you get in the habit of planning. It's not a race to see who gets there first. The important thing is that you start developing healthy habits that will last you a lifetime.

Once you've decided your planning pace, it's time to look at your schedule. Do you have any lunch meetings at work or dinner plans with friends? Are there any evening activities that interfere with the amount of time you have for dinner? For instance, do you get home at 5:30 p.m. and have to be at Cub Scouts at 6:30 p.m.? Do you have time for breakfast?

In examining your schedule, look for activities that get in the way of good health and ask yourself some questions. Do you really need to do everything you're doing? Can you make room for one more home-cooked meal in the week by cutting out an unnecessary activity? Do you have to eat ice cream with your friend, or could you do something different? Do your kids have to do every sport or could you cut out something so the family can eat together?

Now that you know your schedule, you'll be able to plan meals according to the amount of time you have available to cook. You don't want to plan an elaborate meal if you only have an hour to cook and eat. On hectic days, plan something simple. It may be a crock-pot meal, a quick stovetop meal, or something that can be prepared in advance to grab and go. If you know you have to eat a meal out, plan what you are going to eat before you get to the restaurant. Decide in advance to skip the bread or tortilla chips and hide some salad dressing and sea salt in your purse. Plan a lighter meal for dinner if you are going out for lunch.

Soaking grains and legumes need to be on your "to do" list. If you want rice for dinner Wednesday night, you need to begin the soaking before going to bed on Tuesday night or in the morning on Wednesday. If you're having pizza on Friday, you may need to put the flour to soaking on Wednesday night so the crust is ready to prepare Thursday night to be ready for use Friday night. Salads are great when you have limited time to cook, and you can buy pre-washed and cut up vegetables to make it even easier. Beef and chicken can be cut into strips or bite-sized pieces and cooked in a matter of minutes on the stovetop. If you have a day where you only have enough time to eat but not to cook, plan to use leftovers. Just take them out of the freezer a few days in advance, another thing to put on your "to do" list.

You know your pace and your schedule, now it's time to plan what you're eating. We recommend that you start with the cookbook *Nourishing Traditions* by Sally Fallon, but you can also use any cookbook you have on hand. Find recipes you like that fit into the time you have to prepare them and write down the ingredients needed on your shopping list. For recipes that are family favorites, write them on index cards and compile your own cookbook. That way, the recipes are readily available the next time you want to put them on the menu. Take your shopping list with you to the store or use your PDA to keep a record to make sure you get all the supplies you need.

Meals can be planned according to themes. You can designate Monday for beef, Tuesday for chicken, Wednesday for fish, etc., and then add whatever vegetables and side dishes you like. Another option is to plan around cuisines. Monday may be Italian night, Tuesday may be Chinese night, and Wednesday might be Mexican night, etc. You may even want to designate a leftover day where you eat whatever you have left in the refrigerator. The whole family can get involved, with each member taking a day to plan the meal. Mom may plan for Monday, with Dad on Tuesday and Junior on Wednesday. When it comes to planning, there are lots of choices, so pick what works best for you.

When cooking, you may want to make extra for leftovers to cut down on the amount of time spent cooking. The leftover steak you have on Monday night could be put in a steak salad for lunch on Tuesday, or you could make steak fajitas for dinner on Thursday or steak burritos for breakfast on Wednesday. You can also double the recipe and freeze half to use next week when you know you're going to be short on time.

Think outside the box. Eggs aren't just for breakfast, and chicken isn't just for dinner. Omelets or scrambled eggs make a great fast-food dinner and spare you the disease-promoting vegetable oils and soy found in drive-through fast food. The typical American diet is centered on grains, so get out of that box and plan around meats and vegetables. On the Liberation Diet, you will want to limit grains, starchy vegetables, and dried beans and peas, especially at first while you are in the weight-loss phase. Steak with sautéed mushrooms and broccoli is a good example of a delicious low-carb meal. You won't even miss the potato.

Good nutrition starts with a good plan, so set aside some time every week to plan the menus and shop for the ingredients. Plans can be reused to save time down the road, so keep them handy. In addition to helping you lose weight and feel great, meal planning will reduce stress, make meal time more enjoyable and provide more opportunities for your family to eat together. If you don't have a family, meal planning can give you the freedom to invite someone to dinner.

Go shopping

Once you know what foods you are going to prepare, write your list and go shopping. Leave the kids at home if you can, but if you must take them, let them help with selecting fruits and vegetables and have them look for hydrogenated oil and high fructose corn syrup on labels. It's never too early to start teaching good nutrition habits.

Basic rules

Ideally, we would all live on small farms, milk our own cows, grow our own produce, grind our own grain, and make our own bread. But most of us live in big cities with stressful jobs, deadlines, appointments, and budgets. So how do city folk do the Liberation Diet?

1. **Do what you can do and don't worry about what you can't do.** Some of you may not have a source of raw milk or locally grown produce in your area. Don't worry! Just get what you can at the supermarket. Switch from skim milk to whole milk until you are ready or able to get raw milk.

Buy flour at the supermarket instead of grinding your own grain. Start using butter instead of margarine and so on. Every change you make will bring you one step closer to good health and a long life.

2. **Take it one step at a time.** The most important thing to do is get rid of hydrogenated oils, high-fructose corn syrup, processed soy, MSG, and aspartame. Let's say you drink six diet sodas every day. Quitting cold turkey would be a huge step, and one that few could really achieve. Keep in mind that you are on a journey, and every step gets you closer to health. Instead of drinking six sodas, try five sodas each day for a week. Next week, cut down to four sodas. Every week, cut out one soda a day until you are down to drinking one diet soda every day. At this point, substitute a natural soda or some other acceptable beverage for one day of the week. Next week use a substitute for two days and so forth until you are no longer drinking diet soda. Small steps are great, so don't feel bad if you just can't do it all, all at once. If you are stressing out on the program, you are making too many changes too soon.

3. **Don't beat yourself up.** If you mess up and eat something that's not on the list, accept it and move on. You don't have to wait till Monday to start the diet again. Just pick up where you left off and keep moving forward.

4. **Don't eat late.** Finish eating at least three hours before going to bed. Food is fuel, and you don't need fuel to go to bed.

5. **Get at least seven hours of sleep as many days as possible.** Adequate sleep helps maintain proper hormone balance, which makes it easier to take weight off and keep it off.

Kitchen gadgets

There are several tools out there that will make it easier to cook wholesome meals at home. You may have some of these already, or you may need to add them to your Christmas list. We don't want to get sexist, but garages are usually loaded with the latest fix-it gadget and most men are particular about their tools. We want to stress that the kitchen is also a place where good quality tools belong.

Following are kitchen tools, gadgets, and appliances that we recommend:

- **Food processor**
- **Butter bell** (available at William Sonoma)—great for storing butter in hot weather. The butter is kept cool but can be easily spread.
- **Apple corer/slicer**
- **Stainless steel cookware** (no aluminum or Teflon)
- **Chef's, utility, serrated, tomato,** and **cheese knives**
- **Food dehydrator**
- **Tupperware Modular Mates**—for storing and stacking in the pantry or fridge
- **Tupperware FridgeSmarts**—great for keeping produce fresh in the fridge
- **Stoneware**
- **Blender, juicer**
- **Grain grinder**
- **Electric popcorn maker**

You don't have to have all these gadgets to succeed on the Liberation Diet, so it's not necessary to go out and buy everything right now. We have found the above tools to be very useful and just wanted you to be aware of them.

You've got everything you need to succeed in your health and weight loss goals. Enjoy the journey as you get liberated with each step.

Overcoming Obstacles

If you have been following the high-carb, low-fat diet, you will have to overcome cravings and addictions. Some of you may have problems with emotional or mindless eating, and others may need to set boundaries with friends or family. There are a lot of obstacles that can get in the way of our best efforts to lose weight. Identifying those obstacles is crucial so you can develop a plan to overcome them. Here's the how, what, when, where, who, and why of eating.

How

How you eat matters. Do you eat on the run, skip meals, or feel compelled to finish everything on the plate? If you are always eating on the run, you are not taking the time to sit down, give thanks, and eat slowly. Eating on the run generally involves highly processed and refined carbohydrate foods that will keep the weight on. Skipping meals in and of itself is not a bad thing, but if it causes you to raid the pantry or convenience store for anything you can find, it becomes an obstacle. If you can't stand to leave food on a plate, you may be ignoring satiety cues and eating more than you need.

Look for any eating behavior that prevents you from sitting down, chewing slowly, and eating a well-planned, home-cooked meal, and then come up with a plan to overcome the obstacle. For example, if you have to eat everything on the plate, use a smaller plate and put half the amount of food on it. If you are still hungry after the first plate try another plate with even smaller portions on it, but if you are satisfied after the first plate, stop eating. If you eat on the run, evaluate your schedule. Do you have to do everything you are doing? Find a time to fit in a sit-down meal. If you find yourself skipping lunch and pigging out on candy bars by 2:00 p.m., plan to eat a healthy lunch.

What

What you eat is the most important thing, and that's what this book is mostly about. You want to eat real, unprocessed food. Are there any foods you just can't stop eating once you take a bite? If you have cravings for certain foods, you need to find a way to overcome the craving. Do you crave sweets, chocolate, salty foods, crunchy, or creamy foods?

Once you identify any cravings, make sure you don't keep those foods in the house and don't go down that aisle in the supermarket. **If you don't buy it, you can't eat it.** If you can't resist Starbucks, find a driving route that doesn't put you close to one. Fasting any problem food for a two-week period can also help you overcome the craving. Anyone can give up anything for two weeks. By the end of the two weeks, the craving will subside, and you may find that you don't even want that food anymore. Once you are on the Liberation Diet, cravings will subside naturally as your body begins to get all the vital nutrients it needs to stay healthy.

When

When you eat makes a difference, too. If you have a habit of eating right before bedtime, you may find it difficult to lose weight. Make it a rule that you don't eat past a certain time and just stay out of the kitchen after that time. If you can't make it to lunch without breakfast, then eat breakfast, but if you are not a breakfast person, skip that meal. Schedule two or three meals for times in the day when you experience hunger.

Where

Do you pig out at parties, grab the cinnamon rolls at every meeting, or eat in front of the TV? Where do you tend to overeat or indulge in foods that sabotage your weight loss efforts? If you have to attend meetings with food, ask if you can arrange for the meals or offer suggestions. If you don't have a say in the type of food served, bring your own food, or sit so you can't see the food. You don't have to eat something just because someone else provided it. If a coworker always offers candy, politely tell them you are trying to avoid temptation and request that they stop offering the candy to you. Another option is to carry something in both hands so you can't grab any candy. If you tend to eat in front of the TV or computer, make a rule that food stays in the kitchen and dining room.

Who

Some of you may have friends and family that make it difficult to stick to a healthy eating plan. Because the majority of Americans are indoctrinated into the low-fat cult, you will most likely receive some flack from friends or family for following the Liberation Diet. Recognize that you have knowledge they don't have, and they are just parroting what they have heard or read. Be patient and understanding with those who oppose your healthy eating plan. You don't have to get into any arguments, just explain that you are trying something different because the low-fat diet doesn't work for you. Once they see the weight dropping off, they may end up joining you on your health journey.

You do have the right to set boundaries with people. If you are being criticized for your food choices, state politely but firmly that you don't appreciate the critical remarks and you want them to stop. Learn to say "no, thank you" when offered foods that don't fit on your eating plan. If you meet with friends at the local coffee or dessert shop, try to meet at your house or a park instead. Remember, you don't have to eat something just because it is in front of you. It is perfectly acceptable to leave the food on the table.

Don't let anyone bully you into eating something you don't want to eat. You decide what you put in your mouth. It isn't anyone else's business, and you are quite capable of making those choices by yourself.

Why

Hunger should be your cue to eat and satiety should be your cue to stop eating, but many people are cued to eat when rejected, bored, or depressed. If you eat for reasons other than hunger, decide in advance to do something else. For instance, instead of turning to food, you could clean out the junk drawer, read, crochet, putter around in the garden, go for a walk, pray, or put on soothing music. The best tactics get you out of the house and away from food.

Many people overeat because they believe a lot of lies. If anyone says something to you that makes you feel ashamed, guilty, depressed, undeserving, or bad in any way, it is a lie. Identify those lies in your life, reject them, and speak the truth. The truth is, you are beautiful, you have a purpose to carry out, and you deserve to look and feel your best. If you can control your thoughts, you can control your eating.

Money matters

Real food may cost a little more than fake food, but don't let that stop you from eating well. **You need to begin to think about eating the best and healthiest food, not the cheapest.** You are worth the extra expense, and it will save dollars down the road in doctor and hospital bills. Americans spent about 24% of their income on food in the 1950s, but now we spend only 10%. You may be able to get a fast food burger for ninety-nine cents, but what is the quality of that burger?

Evaluate your budget. If you are spending a lot of money on electronics or other gadgets, eating out, or going to movies, maybe you can cut back on those things and use the extra money to buy food that will actually nourish your body. You may need to rearrange your priorities. What you put in your mouth today will effect what you can do in the future. Make health a priority before it's too late.

What if I don't lose weight?

Most people will begin losing weight as soon as they start on the Liberation Diet, but there are some people who may gain weight initially before they start losing. If you have been on a low-fat, low-calorie diet for any length of time, your body may need time to adjust to the change. On a low-fat, low-calorie diet, the body conserves as much energy as it can, and cells are literally starving for nutrients. When you start feeding your body real food with fat soluble vitamins and minerals that are lacking on a low-fat diet, the body stores as much as it can to be used when the supply is no longer there. It takes about two weeks for your body to realize the nutrients are going to keep coming. Once the body is convinced that you are not going back to the low-fat diet, it will conserve only what it needs and the weight will start coming off. You may also find yourself starving and eating a lot of food the first two weeks, and this is perfectly normal. Again, the body is getting all it can while it can. After two weeks, your appetite should return to normal.

Health conditions and medication can also hamper weight loss. If you can't seem to lose weight after a month, have your thyroid and adrenal glands checked as well as hormone levels to see if they are functioning properly. Take inventory of your medications; if any of them cause weight gain, check with your doctor to see if you really need them or if there is an alternative.

Accountability

Having a system of accountability is very important to your long-term success. You can hire a personal trainer, find a like-minded friend, or enlist your spouse to hold you accountable to your eating and exercise plan. If you don't have any support, our online program at www.LiberationFitness.com has a built-in accountability feature that sends a short video of Kevin with an encouraging message to keep you focused on your goals. We also have a "big loser" program in which we encourage you to participate.

Don't look back

Think positively about your outcome! You may have yo-yoed in the past or failed to maintain a healthy weight, but that doesn't mean you will fail on the Liberation Diet. The vast majority of those following the Liberation Diet have not only lost weight, they have maintained that weight loss for years. So, put the past behind you and start with a clean slate. What you did in the past doesn't matter. It only matters what you do from this point on.

References

Chapter 1

1. *The Rise and Fall of Crisco* by Linda Joyce Forristal, CCP, MTA. www.westonaprice.org/motherlinda/fats-crisco.html
2. Daniel PhD, CCN, Kaayla T. *The Whole Soy Story.* New Trends Publishing Inc. 2005. p. 113–119.
3. Bryson, Christopher. *The Flouride Deception.* Seven Stories Press 2004.
4. *The Phosphate Fertilizer Industry: An Environmental Overview* by Michael Connett, Flouride Action Network, May 2003. www.fluoridealert.org/phosphate/overviw.htm
5. USDA Strategic Plan for FY 2005–2010. USDA June 2006. www.ocfo.usda.gov/usdasp/usdasp.htm
6. Griffin, Edward G. *World without Cancer: The story of vitamin B17.* American Media 1997. p. 261–269.

Chapter 2

1. Taubes, Gary. "The Soft Science of Dietary Fat," *Science*, March 2001. www.secondopinion.co.uk/taubes.html
2. Ravnskov MD PhD, Uffe. *The Cholesterol Myths.* New Trends Publishing Inc. Oct 2000.
3. "The Oiling of America" by Mary Enig PhD and Sally Fallon. *Nexus Magazine.* Dec 1998–1999 and Feb 1999–Mar 1999. www.westonaprice.org/knowyourfats/oiling.html
4. D. Kritchevsky, et al, "Effect of Cholesterol Vehicle in Experimental Atherosclerosis," *AM J Physiol*, July–September 1954, 178:30–32.

5. F.H. Mattson, et al, "Effect of Dietary Cholesterol on Serum Cholesterol in Men," *Am J Clin Nutr*, 1972, 25:589

6. "Multiple risk factor intervention trial; risk factor changes and mortality results," *JAMA*, September 24, 1982, 248:(12):1465

7. G. Cristakis, "Effect of the Anti-Coronary Club Program on Coronary Heart Disease Risk-Factor Status," *JAMA*, Nov 7, 1966, 1988 (6):129–35.

8. Ascherio A, et al. Dietary fat and risk of coronary heart disease in men; cohort follow up study in the United States. *BMJ* 1996; 313:313

9. Enig PhD, Mary. *Know Your Fats.* Bethesda Press 2000.

Chapter 3

1. *Porn Flakes; Kellogg, Graham and the crusade for Moral Fiber.* www.ibiblio.org/pub/electronic-publications/stay-free/10/graham.htm

2. Sareen S. Gropper, Jack L. Smith, James L. Groff. *Advanced Nutrition and Human Metabolism.* Wadsworth 2005. p. 72–107.

3. Christian B. Allan, PhD and Wolfgang Lutz, MD, *Life without Bread.* Keats Publishing 2000.

4. Monastyrsky, Konstantin. *Fiber Menace.* Ageless Press 2005.

5. Taubes, Gary, *Good Calories Bad Calories.* Alfred A. Knopf 2007. p. 89–104, 335–449.

6. Cassidy, Marie M, et al., "Effect of chronic intake of dietary fibers on the ultrastructual topography of rat jejunum and colon: a scanning electron microscopy study," *The American Journal of Clinical Nutrition*, 34: February 1981, p. 218–228.

7. Ausman, Lunne M, DSc, "Fiber and Colon Cancer: Does the Current Evidence Justify a Preventive Policy?" *Nutrition Reviews*, 51(2), p. 57–63.

Chapter 4

1. "Low carb diets get thermodynamic defense," by Helen Pearson. www.bioedonline.org/new/news-print.cfm?art=1212
2. "Do calories really count?" www.second-opinions.co.uk/do-calories-really-count.html
3. Taubes, Gary. *Good Calories Bad Calories.* Alfred A. Knopf 2007. p. 229–327.
4. *Science Desk Reference,* New York Public Library, 1995. p. 283.
5. Rothman PhD, Tony. *Instant Physics.* Byron Preiss Visual Publications, Inc. 1995. p. 68–87.

Chapter 5

1. Sareen S. Gropper, Jack L. Smith, James L. Groff, *Advanced Nutrition and Human Metabolism,* Wadsworth 2005. p. 235–239.
2. Salway, J.G., *Metabolism at a Glance,* Blackwell Sciences Ltd 1999. p. 22–23, 60–69.

Chapter 6

1. Blaylock MD, Russell L., *Excitotoxins: the taste that kills,* Health Press 1997.
2. "Why do Americans Overeat? MSG revisited," by Bill Sardi. www.msgtruth.org
3. www.truthinlabeling.org

Chapter 7

1. Ajani et al. "Sodium intake among people with normal and high blood pressure" *Am J Prev Medicine.* Dec 2005: 29: 63–7.
2. Whalley, H. "Salt and hypertension: concensus or controversy?" *Lancet* 1997. Dec 6; 350 (9092):1686.

3. Franco, V., Oparil S. "Salt sensitivity: a determinant of blood pressure, CVD and survival." *J Am Coll Nutr* 2006 June; 25:2475–2555.
4. "Salt and Blood Pressure" www.second-opinions.co.uk/salt-and-hypertension.html
5. www.cspinet.org/salt
6. Pimenta, et al., "Relation of dietary salt and aldosterone to urinary protein excretion in subjects with resistant hypertension," *Hypertension* 2007 Dec 17.

Chapter 8

1. "Eight glasses of water per day," by John Reggars. www.coca.com.au/newsletter/2004/juno411a.htm
2. "Drink at least 8 glasses of water a day—really?" www.eurekalert.org/pub_releases/2002-08/dms-al080802.php
3. www.merck.com/mmpe/sec12/ch156/ch156b.html?qt=total%20water%20losses&alt=sh

Chapter 10

1. American Heart Association. www.americanheart.org/presenter.jhtml?identifier=4591
2. National Center for Health Statistics United States 2006. www.cdc.gov/nchs/hus.htm

Chapter 11

1. www.westonaprice.org
2. Price DDS, Weston A., *Nutrition and Physical Degeneration,* Price-Pottenger Nutrition Foundation 1939.

Chapter 12

1. Price, Weston, DDS, *Nutrition and Physical Degeneration*, 1945, Price-Pottenger Nutrition Foundation, San Diego, CA. Dr. Price referred to vitamins A and D as "fat-soluble activators."
2. Dunne, Lavon J, *Nutrition Almanac*, 3rd ed, 1990, McGraw Hill, New York, NY; Jennings, I W, *Vitamins in Endocrine Metabolism*, 1970, Heineman, London, UK.
3. Solomans, N W, and J Bulox, *Nutrition Reviews*, Jul 1993, 51:199–204.
4. Livera, et al., "Regulation and Perturbation of Testicular Functions by Vitamin A" (Review), *Reproduction* (2002) 124, 173–180.
5. Angler, Natalie, "Vitamins Win Support as Potent Agents of Health," *New York Times*, March 10, 1992.
6. Masterjohn, Chris, *Wise Traditions*, Vol 7, No 1. "Vitamin A on Trial; does vitamin A cause osteoporosis?" p. 25–41.
7. "Clinical Nutrition: A functional Approach," *Institute for Functional Medicine* 2004. p. 97–149.
8. *The Miracle of Vitamin D,* by Krispin Sullivan, CN. www.westonaprice.org/basicnutrition/vitamindmiracle.html

Chapter 13

1. Reported outbreak of food borne illness. www.realmilk.com/foodborne.html
2. Ultra-Pasteurized Milk by Linda Joyce Forristal CCP MTA. www.westonaprice.org/motherlinda/ultra-pasteurizedmilk.html
3. Schmid ND, Ron. *The Untold Story of Milk.* New Trends Publishing 2003.
4. FDA and CDC bias against raw milk. www.westonaprice.org/press/press-12mar07-fda-cdc-raw-milk-reminder.html

Chapter 14

1. Brian and Marianita Jader Shilhavy, *Virgin Coconut Oil,* Tropical Traditions Inc. 2004.
2. Mary Enig PhD and Sally Fallon, *Eat Fat Lose Fat,* Plume 2005.
3. Fallon, Sally, *Nourishing Traditions,* New Trends Publishing Inc. 2001. p. 80–81, 89–91, 112–113, 116–118, 299.
4. "Culturing your food: Pickling and Fermentation," by Anna Bond. www.organicanews.com/news/article.cfm?story_id=93
5. Klaus Kaufmann DSc and Annelies Schoneck, *Making sauerkraut and pickled vegetables at home,* Alive Books. p. 7–12.
6. Katz, Sandor Ellix, *Wild Fermentation,* Chelsea Green Publishing Company 2003. p. 5–27.

Resources

Download a handy one page reference list of good foods/bad foods to keep with you:

www.findyourweigh.com
www.liberationfitness.com

Websites:

www.liberationfitness.com
www.visionarytrainers.com
www.findyourweigh.com
www.realmilk.com: find sources for local raw milk
www.westonaprice.org: accurate nutrition/health information
www.thincs.org: cholesterol skeptics site
www.radiantlifecatalog.com: coconut products, gelatin and more
www.tropicaltraditions.com: coconut products and more
www.organicpastures.com: raw milk
www.vitalchoice.com: salmon and tuna and more
www.uswellnessmeats.com: grass fed beef and bison and more
www.gemcultures.com: kefir grains
www.bodyecology.com: kefir powder, laktano
www.wildernessfamilynaturals.com: kefir powder

Books:

Nourishing Traditions by Sally Fallon

Eat Fat Lose Fat by Dr. Mary Enig and Sally Fallon

The Cholesterol Myths by Uffe Ravnskov

The Whole Soy Story by Kaayla T. Daniel

Real Food by Nina Planck

Good Calories Bad Calories by Gary Taubes

Fiber Menace by Konstantin Monastyrsky

Life without Bread by Christian B. Allan, PhD, and Wolfgang Lutz, MD

Health Myths Exposed by Shane Ellison, M.Sc.

The Fluoride Deception by Christopher Bryson

Excitotoxins: The Taste That Kills by Russell L. Blaylock, MD

Malignant Medical Myths by Joel M. Kauffman, PhD

A Life Unburdened by Richard Morris

Recipes

3 meal per day option

<u>Sunday</u>

Vegetable Omelet

Crock Pot Chicken
Salad with Blended Dressing
Yogurt with Flax and Fruit (optional)

Steak au Poivre
Cauliflower with Cheese

<u>Vegetable Omelet</u>

2 eggs
1 Tablespoon whole milk or cream
Sea salt and pepper to taste
½ Tablespoon butter
2 Tablespoons chopped mushroom
2 Tablespoons chopped onion
1 ounce shredded raw milk cheese

Whisk eggs, cream, salt, and pepper until well blended. Heat butter in pan. Add eggs, stirring frequently. When eggs are no longer runny, add vegetables and cheese and cook till done.

rock-Pot Chicken (Save some for salad Monday)

1 whole chicken
4 Tablespoons melted butter
Real Salt brand season-all salt and pepper to taste

Rub butter on chicken and sprinkle with season-all salt and pepper.
Place in 5 to 6 quart crock-pot and cook about 6 hours on low.

Salad with Blended Dressing

1 cup romaine lettuce
3 baby carrots, sliced
3 cherry tomatoes
¼ cup sliced cucumber
2 Tablespoons chopped walnuts
2 Tablespoons Blended Dressing

Combine all ingredients.

Blended Dressing

¼ cup coconut oil
¼ cup extra virgin olive oil
¼ cup unrefined sesame oil (not toasted)
¼ cup balsamic vinegar
1 Tablespoon Dijon mustard
¼ teaspoon garlic powder
¼ teaspoon onion powder
Pepper to taste
Stevia to taste (optional)

Mix all ingredients and pour over salad. Keep refrigerated but take out of fridge 30 minutes before using.

Yogurt with Flax and Fruit

1 cup whole milk plain yogurt
½ teaspoon vanilla extract
Few drops liquid stevia
1 Tablespoon ground flaxseed
½ cup blueberries, raspberries, strawberries, or blackberries

Mix yogurt, vanilla and stevia until well blended. Stir in flaxseed and blueberries.

Steak au Poivre (make enough for salad Tuesday)

4 (6 ounces each) tenderloin steaks
1 teaspoon sea salt
4 teaspoons fresh coarsely ground black pepper
1 Tablespoon butter
5 Tablespoons Cognac or Brandy
3 Tablespoons Dijon mustard
2/3 cup half and half
2 Tablespoons butter

Coat steaks with salt and pepper. Add butter to hot pan, melt and add steaks. Turn once and cook to desired degree of doneness. Remove steak and reserve on warm plate. Add Cognac to the pan and let sit for 5 seconds and light with match. Flame should burn out after 10 seconds. Stir over medium high heat. Reduce heat to low and slowly stir Dijon and half and half into drippings. Whisk in remaining butter and stir for 2 minutes until sauce becomes thick. Pour sauce over steak and serve.

Cauliflower with Cheese

1 head cauliflower cut up
1 Tablespoon butter
2 ounces shredded cheddar cheese

Steam cauliflower until desired texture reached. Drain and stir in butter and cheese.

Monday

Fried eggs with Cheese

Chicken Salad
Yogurt with Flax (optional)

Grilled Salmon with Basil Pistachio Butter
Parmesan Asparagus
1 ounce raw milk Cheese

Fried Eggs with Cheese

2 farm fresh eggs
1 Tablespoon butter
1 ounce raw milk cheese

Spread butter on hot griddle. Crack eggs onto griddle. Cook till done. Flip once. Serve with cheese.

Chicken Salad

¼ cup safflower oil mayonnaise
¼ cup sour cream

½ Tablespoon Dijon mustard
½ teaspoon garlic powder
½ teaspoon onion powder
Sea salt and Pepper to taste
3 cups left-over chopped or shredded chicken
1 bunch green onions
1 cup lettuce or mixed greens
2 Tablespoons slivered almonds
½ apple, cut up
2 Tablespoons blended dressing

Mix first 6 ingredients until well blended. Stir in chicken and onions. Pile 1 cup chicken salad on lettuce. Add almonds, apples and dressing.

Yogurt with Flax

1 cup whole fat plain yogurt
½ teaspoon vanilla extract
Pinch stevia
1 Tablespoons ground flaxseed

Mix first 3 ingredients and stir in flaxseed.

Grilled Salmon with Basil Pistachio Butter

1 pound salmon filets
Sea salt and pepper
3/4 cup chopped fresh basil leaves
1/3 cup shelled pistachios (about 1/8 pound unshelled)
2 teaspoons fresh lime juice
½ Tablespoon minced garlic
¼ cup softened butter

Heat grill and oil grate. Cut salmon into 4 portions and season both sides with salt and pepper. Place basil, pistachios, lime juice, and garlic in blender and pulse until pistachios and basil are finely chopped. Use spatula to scrape down sides. Remove mixture to a small bowl and stir in softened butter. Grill salmon 4 inches above medium heat. Cook filets 5 to 6 minutes per side or until salmon is just cooked through. Place on plates and top with basil mix.

Parmesan Asparagus

18 steamed asparagus spears
1 Tablespoon butter
1 Tablespoon parmesan cheese

Cut off woody ends of asparagus and steam until tender. Melt butter on top and mix in parmesan cheese.

Tuesday

Scrambled Eggs with Cheese

Steak Salad
Yogurt with Flax and Fruit (optional)

Roasted Turkey Breast
Broccoli
1 ounce raw milk cheese

Scrambled Eggs with Cheese

2 eggs
1 Tablespoon milk
Sea salt and pepper to taste
1 ounce shredded cheddar cheese

Beat eggs, milk, salt and pepper until well blended. Melt butter in hot skillet. Add eggs and cook, stirring frequently. When almost done, add cheese and cook till desired doneness.

Steak Salad

3 ounces leftover steak
1 cup mixed greens
3 cherry tomatoes
3 baby carrots, sliced
3 sliced radishes
2 Tablespoons Blended Dressing

Mix all ingredients and enjoy. (Other vegetables can be added or substituted)

Roasted Turkey Breast (save some for Wednesday lunch)

Large turkey breast with bone and skin
4 Tablespoons melted butter
Real Salt brand Season All Salt
Pepper

Rub turkey with butter and sprinkle with season all salt and pepper. Put in roasting or baking pan and bake at 350 degrees F about 1 ¼ to 2 hours.

Broccoli

1 head broccoli, cut up
1 Tablespoon butter
Sea salt and pepper to taste

Steam broccoli. Drain and stir in butter. Add salt and pepper to taste.

Wednesday

Omelet
Turkey Salad
Yogurt with Flax and Fruit (optional)
1 ounce raw milk cheese

Meatloaf
Green Beans
1 ounce raw milk cheese

Omelet

2 eggs
½ Tablespoon butter
1 ounce shredded cheese
Vegetables of choice

Heat butter in skillet. Mix eggs and pour into pan. When cooked slightly, add cheese and vegetables on half of eggs and fold other half over. Cook till done, flipping as needed.

Turkey Salad

3 ounces leftover turkey
1 cup lettuce or mixed greens
2 Tablespoons walnuts
2 Tablespoons Blended Dressing

Mix all ingredients.

Meatloaf (Save some for lunch Thursday)

1 medium onion, chopped
2 peeled and chopped carrots
8 chopped baby portabella mushrooms
4 Tablespoons butter
¼ teaspoon red pepper flakes
1 teaspoon thyme
1 teaspoon sea salt
Pepper to taste
2 pounds ground beef, bison or venison
½ pound beef liver, ground
1 egg, beaten
¼ cup organic ketchup

Sauté vegetables in butter until soft. Add spices. Mix meat, egg and vegetables. Put in loaf pan and ice with ketchup. Bake at 350 degrees F for 1 ½ hours.

<u>Green Beans</u>

1 cup steamed green beans
½ Tablespoon butter
Sea salt and pepper to taste

Steam green beans, drain and mix with butter, salt and pepper.

<u>Thursday</u>

Guacamole Eggs
Sausage

Taco Salad
Yogurt with Flax and Fruit (optional)

Shrimp in Turmeric and Garlic Butter
Lemon Spinach
1 ounce raw milk cheese

<u>Guacamole Eggs</u>

2 eggs
¼ cup half and half
1 Tablespoon butter
2 Tablespoons guacamole
1 ounce shredded cheese

Mix eggs and half and half. Heat butter in hot skillet and pour in eggs. When nearly done, add guacamole and cheese.

Sausage

2 uncured sausages cooked according to package instructions.

Taco Salad

Leftover meatloaf, crumbled
1 cup romaine lettuce
1 ounce shredded cheese
3 cherry tomatoes
3 jumbo black olives
2 Tablespoons sour cream
2 Tablespoons salsa

Mix sour cream and salsa and pour over remaining ingredients.

Shrimp in Turmeric Garlic Butter

12 ounces fresh or frozen peeled and de-veined shrimp
4 Tablespoons butter
4 cloves garlic
½ teaspoon turmeric
2 Tablespoons chopped parsley
2 Tablespoons cooking sherry

Thaw frozen shrimp. In large skillet, heat butter over medium-high heat. Add shrimp, garlic, and turmeric and sauté until shrimp turns pink (about 1 to 3 minutes). Stir in parsley and sherry.

Lemon Spinach

2 bunches spinach, washed
2 Tablespoons butter
2 garlic cloves, minced
¼ teaspoon red pepper flakes
Juice of 1 or 2 lemons

Sauté garlic in butter. Add spinach and red pepper flakes and cook just till wilted. Mix in lemon juice and serve.

Friday

Salmon Cream Cheese Rolls
1 ounce raw milk cheese

Corned Beef Wrap
Yogurt with Flax and Fruit (optional)

Herbed Spare Ribs
Fried Zucchini
1 ounce raw milk cheese

Salmon Cream Cheese Rolls (From Eat Fat Lose Fat by Sally Fallon and Mary Enig, page 236)

3 Tablespoons cream cheese
1 teaspoon dried dill
Sea salt and pepper to taste
2 ounces smoked wild salmon

Mix cream cheese with dill, salt and pepper. Spread over salmon and roll up. Slice into ½ inch rounds.

Corned Beef Wrap

2 ounces corned beef
3 shredded baby carrots
½ cup sauerkraut
1 ounce shredded Swiss cheese
2 teaspoons butter
2 lettuce leafs

Butter lettuce leafs and stuff with remaining ingredients. Roll up and eat.

Herbed Spare Ribs

2 pounds pork spare ribs in serving pieces
4 Tablespoons melted butter
1½ cloves garlic, minced
½ teaspoon paprika
½ teaspoon sea salt
½ teaspoon dried rosemary
¼ teaspoon oregano
¼ teaspoon marjoram

Put ribs in 2 baking pans. Cover and bake at 350 degrees F for 45 minutes or until juices run clear and meat is tender. Combine remaining ingredients and brush over meat. Grill over medium heat 7 minutes on each side, brushing frequently with herbs.

<u>Fried Zucchini</u>

Fry sliced zucchini in 1 to 2 Tablespoons butter about 2 to 5 minutes. Season with sea salt and pepper per taste.

Saturday

Veggie Scramble

Hotdogs
Coleslaw with Creamy Dressing
Yogurt with Flax
½ Apple

Easy Fried Chicken
Green Cauliflower
1 ounce raw milk cheese

<u>Veggie Scramble</u>

2 eggs
1 Tablespoon milk
Sea salt and pepper to taste
1 Tablespoon butter
¼ bell pepper in strips or chopped
¼ cu chopped onion
1 ounce shredded cheese

Mix eggs, milk, salt, and pepper until well blended. Add butter to hot skillet and pour egg mixture in. Stir constantly. Add bell pepper, onion and cheese and cook till done.

Hotdogs

Cook 2 uncured hotdogs according to package directions.

Coleslaw (From Nourishing Traditions by Sally Fallon page 195)

1 head cabbage, shredded
2 peeled and grated carrots
1 small finely chopped red onion
1 tablespoon celery seeds
1 cup Creamy Dressing

Mix all ingredients and serve.

Creamy Dressing (From Nourishing Traditions by Sally Fallon page 131)

1 teaspoon Dijon mustard
2 Tablespoons plus 1 teaspoon raw wine vinegar
½ cup extra virgin olive oil
1 Tablespoon expeller expressed flax oil
¼ cup crème fraiche

Mix thoroughly.

Easy Fried Chicken

6 chicken legs
¼ cup melted butter
Real Salt brand season-all salt
Pepper to taste
¼ cup palm oil

Place chicken in baking dish. Pour butter over chicken and season with season-all salt and pepper. Bake at 350 degrees F for about 30 minutes. Heat oil in skillet on medium high heat and place chicken in hot oil. Use cover or splatter guard. Cook about 2 to 3 minutes on each side until skin is crisp.

Green Cauliflower

1 head green cauliflower, cut up
1 Tablespoon butter
Sea salt and pepper to taste

Steam cauliflower until tender. Drain and mix in butter, salt and pepper.

2 meal per day option: Use recipes from 3 meal per day option and adjust according to notes below. You may need larger portions than the 3 meal plan.

Sunday

Vegetable Omelet
Yogurt with Flax and Fruit (optional)

Steak au Poivre
Cauliflower with cheese
Salad with Blended Dressing

Vegetable Omelet

Use 3 eggs instead of 2 and increase amount of vegetables if desired.

Monday

Fried eggs with Cheese
Yogurt with Flax and Fruit (optional)

Grilled Salmon with Basil Pistachio Butter
Parmesan Asparagus
Salad with Blended Dressing
1 ounce raw milk cheese

Tuesday

Scrambled Eggs with Cheese
Yogurt with Flax and Fruit (optional)

Roasted Turkey Breast
Broccoli
Salad with Blended Dressing
1 ounce raw milk cheese

Wednesday

Omelet
Yogurt with Flax and Fruit (optional)

Meatloaf
Green beans
Salad with Blended Dressing
1 ounce raw milk cheese

Omelet

Use 3 eggs.

Thursday

Guacamole Eggs
Sausage or Leftover Meatloaf
Yogurt with Flax and Fruit (optional)

Shrimp in Garlic Butter
Lemon Spinach
Salad with Blended Dressing
1 ounce raw milk cheese

Friday

Salmon Cream Cheese Rolls
2 ounces raw milk cheese
Yogurt with Flax and Fruit (optional)

Herbed Spare Ribs
Fried Zucchini
Salad with Blended Dressing

Salmon Cream Cheese Rolls

Use 4 Tablespoons cream cheese and 3 ounces salmon.

Saturday

Veggie Scramble
Yogurt with Flax and Fruit (optional)

Easy Fried Chicken
Coleslaw with Creamy Dressing
Green Cauliflower

Veggie Scramble

Use 3 eggs and 2 Tablespoons shredded cheese.

Success Stories

Healthy baby and slimmer hubby

After many failed attempts, Simon's wife, Brigitte came to us to help her and Simon achieve their dream of becoming parents. After Kevin's one-on-one nutritional counseling and *The Liberation Diet*, Brigitte successfully conceived and nine months later gave birth to a beautiful healthy baby girl (isn't she adorable?)!

Congratulations to the happy couple!

Brigitte and Simon Black, Concord, California

Healthy baby Brianna

Chubby Hubby loses 75 pounds

I had been trying to lose weight for years. I had been working out 5 days a week for years, but my weight just seemed to creep up out of control before my eyes. I tried listening to doctors to "eat 6 times a day" but my weight still either went up, or stayed the same. After listening to Kevin and what he in-

structed me to do concerning my eating habits, I lost 75 pounds in 9 months, and I went from a 44 inch waist, to a loose 36 inch waist. Even through out the holiday season, I've managed to keep my weight loss maintained. Since then I've never looked back, and I'll never buy larger clothes again.

Thanks Kevin!"

-Simon Black - Concord, CA.

Lost 86 pounds and counting!

Dentist loses 44 pounds in 4 months

I would like to take a moment to thank Kevin Brown of Liberation Fitness for transforming my life this past summer. I had really fallen into a terrible pattern of eating poorly, not exercising and letting my overall health take a back seat to my new dental practice. As a result, I gained lots of weight over the last two years and experienced a noticeable decline in energy and increase in stress. That all changed when I decided to hire Kevin.

I met with Kevin late June and found him to be not only knowledgeable about weight training/exercise but also well-versed in nutrition. He started me on a diet and workout program and the results were amazing. I lost over thirty pounds in three months and feel and look great. I have more energy to deal with the stress associated with my profession and have become an overall healthier, stronger person.

I can, without reservation, recommend Kevin's program to anybody who is interested in getting healthier and improving their quality of life. Before I met Kevin, I was lazy and plain old fat. Now Kevin calls me his biggest loser. I lost nine pounds in the first week. Altogether I have lost approximately forty-four pounds—and it was quite easy!

Within four months, I had reached my goal. It was just good eating and good exercising. Most of my patients and friends are just shocked. They ask: How did you do it, and how can I do it? Now everything is better. Kevin is always on top of things, and he explains things with scientific evidence. Being a dentist, I'm kind of a scientist, and Kevin takes away the fallacy and gives me reality. Before when I was sopping, I'd go right in a store and come right back out again. I'd blame it on European sizes. Now I walk out with two bags. I would definitely recommend the Liberation Fitness Program.

It's not a difficult program. You don't need to weigh things. You don't need to count things. You need to eat healthy, exercise and have a postitive mental attitude. Now I'm looking forward to any reunion—high school, college, dental school. I look forward to seeing people who haven't seen me in years. People used to look at me and not see me. I was invisible. Now they see the real me—and I'm thrilled!

Victoria M. Caldwell, DMD

Executive Assistant loses 30 pounds and feels fabulous

I hadn't realized how much weight I had gained until I went to visit my doctor when I wasn't feeling well. When I stepped on the scale, I couldn't believe it! I wasn't fat, but I knew I had begun to pack on some excess weight. I didn't like the direction this was headed—to say the least! In addition, Diabetes runs in my family, and I did not want to become another victim. I had also recently gotten engaged and wanted to look fabulous for my engagement party and wedding.

So, I decided to be *proactive*. I decided if I start now when I'm young, then perhaps I won't fall victim to the illnesses that have plagued many of my family members. So, after speaking with my fiancé, he suggested I go see Kevin. Kevin educated me about my eating habits and the importance of whole food nutrition along with exercise. I took notes on what I should be eating and not eating, listened intently to the message, and signed up for training with someone who turned out to be an awesome trainer.

What really impacted me the most in the message was learning that if you really listen and follow this diet and adapt it as part of your lifestyle, you can reverse some of the damage you've done to your body and your health! After a week of the Liberation Diet and working out with Visionary Trainers I lost seven pounds. Me being the ultimate skeptic, I was flabbergasted and ecstatic at the same time! Week two I lost six pounds, and continued to lose a few pounds a week until I finally achieved my goal weight after two and half months! I lost a total of thirty pounds! What an excuse to go out shopping!

Now, it's almost two years later. I looked fabulous at my wedding, have maintained the weight loss I and feel better than ever! I used to get sick a lot, colds, the flu, throat infections, etc. Since I made this diet a part of my everyday life (The Liberation Lifestyle I like to call it), I have not been sick.

People in my office have been sick many, many times, and luckily, I have not been one of them. Prior to the Liberation Diet I most definitely would get sick! Sure, it could be coincidence, but *I don't think so*! Looking ahead to the future, I'm so glad to have learned about the importance of whole food nutrition—it plays an important role in family planning.

I can take what I've learned and be confident that when my husband and I decide to start a family, the children will be as healthy as can be!

Lisa N.
Age: 29
Occupation: Executive Assistant
Lost 30 pounds!

Kevin is a money manager whose stressful job and frequent work-related client entertaining made it easy to form bad habits where fitness was concerned.

Realizing the need for a change, Kevin turned to Liberation Fitness. His success has inspired his entire family.

I've worked with Kevin for 18 months and I've lost 20-plus pounds. When you become physically fit, you feel physically terrific. I work in a stressful industry. I'm a money manager, and with the rigors of the job, I was putting on a lot of weight. I work in a lot of social settings with food and drink. I wasn't feeling real well. Now I'm much more enthusiastic and passionate and clients pick up on that. I went to buy a pair of jeans and I was a size smaller in the waist.

Before: **After:**

30 Pound Loss

This program is contagious – when I started to lose weight, my wife started to do it to. And now our kids are eating healthier.

The entire family is feeling better. There's no need for little blue pills in our house.

I would absolutely recommend Kevin's program to anyone.

We are so bombarded in our society with bad lifestyle choices and bad food choices.

Kevin's program cuts through the clutter and helps you to make the right choices.

There was a time when I was younger that I could eat a 2 lb. hoagie and go to bed and lose weight. Now I just drive past a hoagie restaurant and look inside and put on weight – but Kevin has me eating right, and certainly exercising right.

Kevin Supka
Age 50
Occupation: Financial Planner
Lost: 30 Pounds

Longtime exerciser finally gets results

Just because someone routinely exercises does not mean they will realize their full potential. Hear how this sixty-two-years-young woman incorporated the Liberation Fitness nutrition diet plan and finally realized the results she had been waiting for. She may be sixty-two, but she feels forty.

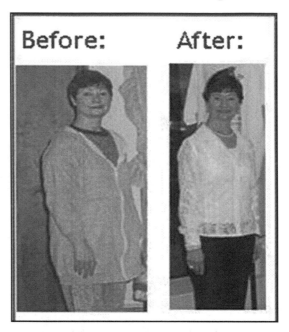

I always exercised, walking marathons, walking on a treadmill, and bowling, but I wasn't perfect in the field of nutrition. Kevin put me on the Liberation Diet, and helped me with essential minerals. Within a week I could feel the difference. I am now a role model in the community. I lost almost twenty-five pounds. I'll be sixty-two next month and I feel like I am in my forties. No one believes I'm my age. I call the Liberation Program the Fountain of Youth.

The decision to train with Kevin of Liberation Fitness was one of the best decisions of my life. He helped me accomplish in a few weeks what I couldn't accomplish in a lifetime of trying. Kevin created a customized nutrition, exercise, and supplement program for me, and it is producing really impressive (and fast!) results. I look better, feel better, and am extremely pleased with my progress and performance. I actually look forward to my workouts because I feel so great afterwards. Kevin is truly an expert in his field, and he has made a real difference in my life. Not only is he an excellent trainer and health and fitness coach, but he has a very caring and understanding manner and is a pleasure to work with. Our relationship has been so very beneficial to me. I plan to continue as his client for a long, long time.

Pat K.
New Jersey
Age: 62
Occupation: Office Manager
Lost: 26 pounds and has maintained for over 3 years

Mother and daughter get liberated

A Mothers' quest to help her daughter battle obesity leads to a solution for both. Hear how Liberation Fitness helps this family lose 121 pounds collectively and create a better lifestyle for both mother and daughter.

"I lost seventy-seven pounds" "I lost forty-four pounds"

Mother: My daughter was obese. We tried everything. I took her

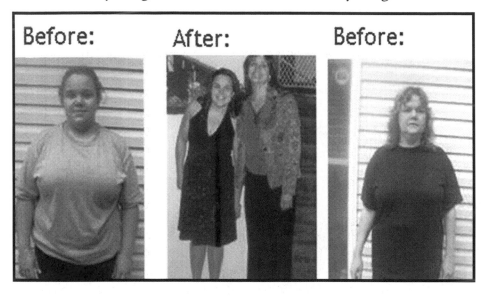

to a nutritionist. That didn't work. We tried Weight Watchers. That didn't work. We went to Curves. Nothing was working. Not until we tried Kevin's Liberation Program did we see any results. Now she looks so much better and so much prettier.

Daughter: My friends are so proud that I could accomplish something like this. On Kevin's Liberation Program, I lost seventy-seven pounds. It was something I had to do. At times it was hard, but it was worth it.

Mother: Before, a flight of stairs was a killer for me. I couldn't go up stairs without huffing and puffing. Kevin's program changed the way I eat. I don't eat chemicals and fake sugars. The diet energizes me. I lost forty-four pounds. Kevin's program doesn't only tell you how to exercise; it tells you how to eat.

Daughter: Now I have so much more confidence. My friends at school compliment me all the time. And I was concerned my mom was unhealthy, and I love my mom. Kevin's Liberation Program changed my life.

Louri D.
Age: 47
Occupation: Dental Assistant
Lost: 44 pounds

Jaime D.
Age: 16
Occupation: Student
Lost: 77 pounds

Computer consultant gets the help he needs

I knew I needed some help. I consider myself lucky to have received a phone call from Kevin Brown one afternoon after not being at the gym for a few months. At the time I weighed in at about 200 pounds. I was twenty-five pounds overweight. I went into training with Kevin. I now find myself six months later in the best shape I have been in my life.

Several things started to happen after the first few weeks. I found myself feeling better, thinking more clearly and having more energy. The best was yet to come.

Kevin not only set up a personal training program that fit my needs but added something that I had not considered—not just a diet but a complete educational nutrition program. I believe that his expert guidance in getting the right information about physical fitness plus the nutrition made all the difference.

Now I feel great about the way I look, but on a deeper level I feel really healthy. Kevin's deep conviction that exercise and nutrition can help his clients in all aspects of their lives will affect anyone who trains with him. My blood pressure, which had been high, is now normal, I have lost twenty-five pounds and six inches around my waist, the daily indigestion is gone, and people around me compliment me on my appearance. That vague feeling I had about not being in control of my own health is gone.

Bob McGuire
Computer Consultant
Philadelphia, Pennsylvania

Undisciplined couch potatoes lose weight

Together they were looking to get in shape. Hear how this publisher and lawyer are enjoying life better thanks to Liberation Fitness.

Richard: I was more active playing tennis and golf, but I didn't have the discipline to be really fit. Discipline is part of what is necessary. The Liberation Program has given me the discipline to exercise regularly. I'm sixty-three years old, and I started seeing definition in my arms and legs. The energy you get from working out is just incredible. It's a very easy program to sell because of the benefits and the results—the way I look and the way I feel. The Liberation Program made me look better and feel better.

Katherine: I was a couch potato. I tended to read and do sedentary activities. But I worried about middle-aged women issues like bone density. I have recommended the program to many people. It gets results. My husband and I are thrilled to be working with Kevin Brown of Liberation Fitness. I started with Kevin a year ago; my husband, seeing the improvement in my muscle tone and energy level, joined the workout schedule six months ago. It's now an essential part of our lives. Kevin knows just how hard to push us, when to crank it up, and when to lay back. He's gentle, but firm, about the need to eat right. As a result of his guidance, I find

myself getting the right amount of exercise, eating better, and taking my vitamins and minerals. Before I started working with Kevin, I had never done any weight training. I just had another bone density test, and the doctor was pleased to report a noticeable improvement. I attribute it to the workouts and the minerals. Kevin's the best.

Richard B.
Age: 64
Occupation: Newspaper
Publisher
Lost: 11 pounds

Katherine H.
Age: 54
Occupation: Attorney
Lost: 4 pounds

"I feel great, and I look 10 years younger."

Jenny W
Riverton New Jersey,
Age: 38,
Event Coordinator
Lost 27 pounds

New mom finally sheds maternity clothes

When I got pregnant, I gained sixty pounds. My husband was like, "What happened to you?" After the baby was born, I was stuck. I was still wearing maternity clothes. It was horrible. I work with all guys, and they were asking me: "Are you having another one?" So I started the Liberation program, and I noticed a change right away. I had back pains from picking up the baby, and the back pains went away. And then I wasn't wearing maternity clothes anymore. I could fit into smaller clothes. Now the guys are work are all like, "Look at you! Look at your butt." I get a lot of catcalls and whistles. Doing the Liberation Program isn't difficult. I look forward to it. When I miss a session I feel miserable.

Stacy M.
Reading, Pennsylvania
Age: 35
Homemaker
Lost: 15 pounds

Stay-at-home mom gets in shape

After I had my third child, I wanted to get back into shape. I noticed results right away. I was able to get back into my jeans after three weeks. My family began to notice definition in my arms, and my legs toning up. Everything started to get more fun. For women who have kids, it's just so much easier to work out at home. If I had to work out at a gym, I'd never do it. I'd bring my kids to the basement with me. I'm liberated and you can be, too!

Melissa H.
Age: 35
Occupation: Marketing
Lost: 5 pounds

My father died at fifty-nine and his father at fifty-eight, and a lot had to do with weight. I was determined not to let that happen to me. I wanted to make a positive change. I was looking for more than just exercise. I was looking for help with diet, too, because if you don't put all the pieces together, you are never going to meet your goal. Now my children see a whole new me. My youngest is very athletic. He's a distance biker. I can ride with him now and almost keep up. My wife says this is the old me she first knew. I had a get-together with a college roommate, and he was jealous. He had put on weight and let himself go. When you get up in the morning and don't want to see yourself naked, it's time for a change. When you see all the changes, it's pretty impressive. It's hard work, but it's worth it. If I have to miss a day, I really do miss it. It's something I really enjoy doing.

Benjamin H.
Age: 52
Occupation: Chief Financial
Officer
Lost: 75 pounds

Rekindle your love life with The Liberation Diet

Janine: I am twenty years younger. I wanted us both to be out-standing. Now our family tells us we look great. I lost seventeen pounds and I'm still losing. I have a lot more energy. We've recommended the Liberation Program to all our patients. I'm going to do this for life.

Sid: I was getting old. I was sixty-six and my flexibility was poor. My balance wasn't good. I had adipose around my belly. I used to be a distance runner, but in recent years I had done nothing. I felt like I was an old man. I looked older than I am. Now she looks hot. She looks like when I met her eleven years ago. I chase her all over the house—and she lets me catch her! When you are fit it makes your whole life better. It made our love life better!

Dr. Stanton
Age: 46
Occupation: Dentist
Lost: 23 pounds

Dr. Silverman
Age: 66
Occupation: Dentist
Lost: 5 pounds

Motivational speaker and business coach lost 45 pounds in 5 months

Before I met Kevin, I weighed 240 pounds. I wasn't feeling good. I couldn't fit into my clothes. I was disappointed in my appearance. I'm a success coach, and I was highly motivated to get into shape. Then I started working with Kevin's Liberation Program. I went from 240 pounds to 203 pounds in forty days. And then down to 198 in another fifteen days. And then down to 195 pounds.

I've lost forty-five pounds in five months. It was all due to Kevin's program. I went from a size 46 to a 42 suit coat. I had to get all new clothes. Now I'm eating right and exercising right. Now my goal is to maintain my new weight forever. In fact, I'm thinking of going to 189 just for grins. I am in better shape today than I have been in twenty years. I played ball till I was forty-seven years old, and I am in better shape now than I was then. I've recommended Kevin's Liberation Program to anyone who is serious about getting physically fit. Kevin's program is a home run.

Bruce M.
Age: 57
Occupation: Business Coach
Lost: 50 pounds

Best human practices and practical concepts

Dear Mr. Brown,

As you know, at the start of this New Year, my husband and I decided we needed to make some major adjustments in our lives. We had put on a tremendous amount of weight, were constantly tired, not getting our housework done and we were eating for recreational purposes. Worse yet, our five year-old daughter was beginning to pick up all of our bad habits.

One night we were watching 'The Biggest Loser' and started talking about how we might apply these theories in our lives. In the past, we have subscribed to a wide variety of fad diets and exercise machines. Nothing was working and even when we experienced short term results, the weight gain came on full-force shortly thereafter. We realized we needed some solid guidance and support to get through this. We decided there would be no more reading, no more experimenting and certainly no more roller coaster effect!

We searched the internet and were blessed to find you via Visionary Trainers. Within 1 week, as you may recall, you had us both on a track for a healthy and much more meaningful lifestyle. You patiently and passionately took the time to explain your theories and systems to us in a way that we could understand. Kevin, your plan makes sense. It is designed around best human practices and practical concepts versus the modern theories of substitute, replacement and deprivation. This is the underlying reason it is working for us.

We have been faithful to the Liberation Diet which is NOT a diet at all but about making smart choices and understanding the source of our foods. Still, no weight loss plan comes without exercise.

Our personal trainer, Sherri, that you hand-picked for us through Visionary Trainers has been coming to our home 3 times each week to educate us in proper and results-oriented physical exercise. Sherri motivates us and keeps us on our toes. She is someone we can no longer live without! There is no greater motivation than a devoted and caring professional knocking at your door at 5:30 in the morning to get you revved up for your day.

Within 3 weeks on this program, I lost 10 pounds (5.3% body weight) and my husband lost 15 pounds (6.5% body weight). We are not tired but full of energy. We are not agonizing over a diet and food deprivation but loving our meals and feeling very fulfilled. We are not spending any more money on this meal and exercise plan than we were before because we are not eating out anymore. Instead we go out for activity and pure entertainment. People are noticing the transformation and it feels great! We continue to lose weight, our skin has better tone and our faces are rejuvenating.

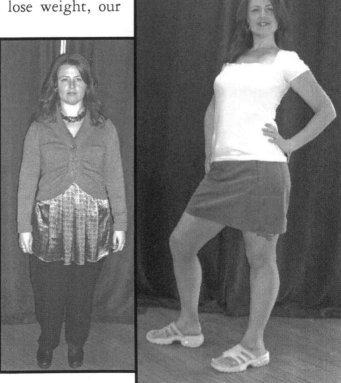

Still, there are so many other benefits to share. We now have energy to play actively with our daughter rather than sending her to her play room or the television. We are getting our housework done and then some. I personally have been so energized and crisp at the office that my productivity has increased by almost 25%. Whereas I was getting my work done within the day before, I now find myself over producing and/or asking for more. My husband and I are getting 'charged' up again about each other as we were early in our marriage. Most importantly, we are now spending daily quality time together. We are exercising, cooking, working on house projects, etc. Our daughter is learning the system and excited about it. She enjoys participating in our exercise regimen where she can. To put it quite simply, we feel great, we are looking great and we are having FUN again!

Kevin, we could never have pulled this off without you. We are so grateful for you and this program. Thank you for giving us our lives back.

With much fondness and gratitude,

Michele Tate - Lost 40 lbs.
Yardley PA

Initiating a fitness program at the age of 61 and with many years of non-athletic lifestyle, my expectations were almost laughable.

I signed up with Visionary Trainers in January, 2008; with a goal to lose a middle-age "spare tire" and build some muscular defini-

tion. Initiating a fitness program at the age of 61 and with many years of non-athletic lifestyle, my expectations were almost laughable. I started working out 1/24/08 (5'-11" and weighing about 166 to 168#), working out three times a week, 2 workouts with the trainer and one more solo. You could not say that I was overweight, but I was definitely out of shape, with a distinct belly. Within the first three months, I started shedding body fat and my weight dropped to 162#. But then, I started gaining weight again (alarming at first!) and learned that I was now building muscle and gaining mass. I reached 175.0# on 7/23 and about a week later, I started to run 3-days/week (alternating days with

the weight training), following a 10-week plan for slowly building up the joints and stamina to jog 3 miles. In reality, it took me many more weeks to reach the 3-mile goal... just a week ago in mid-October. On 9/9 I weighed in at 172.0# (the few pounds loss attributed to running) and today (10/15/08) at 169#. The "belly" (not the waist) started at 39.0" back on 1/24 and since 9/24 has held steady at 35.0"... you can even see some abs muscle definition, though far from a 6-pack! The upper arms (biceps/triceps area) are over 2" bigger than when I started, and the chest has grown 2.5" to 41.5". The thighs don't show as much change (an inch max and holding steady due to running, but hard & solid), and calves show about 3/4" increase. Yesterday, I had to wear a suit and tie and was amazed at how much my body has changed. The pants were loose, but the jacket was tight around my back and shoulders and the sleeves (from the growth of chest, back and shoulders) were too short. I guess I should look at

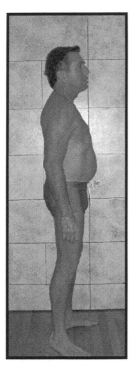 

that as all good! I'm hoping to continue on to improve to the next level, and am mixing in some bodyweight training to further the physical and my personal challenge.

Honestly, I must admit that when I looked at all the pictures (and compared them side-by-side), I was pleasantly surprised. I took the pictures myself using a tripod and the timer feature on the camera, so I was also able to take shots from angles one normally cannot see of one's own body. If I may say so myself, I've come a long way!

Best regards,
Guillermo Vivas
Trenton NJ

Nurse begins to eat like a tiger

Dear Kevin,

After hearing you give a lecture on the Liberation Diet in Virginia, I began to follow your teaching and "eat like a Tiger". I have lost 23 pounds so far and the weight is still coming off! Thanks for helping me *"get liberated"*!

Maggie Fletcher – Lost 23 pounds
Shenandoah Valley, Va.

Doctor recommended

As Executive Vice President of a medical consulting firm, my 100-hour work weeks are more the rule than the exception. So when I decided two months ago to get serious about a fitness program that would become a routine part of my life, I came to a conclusion that initially seemed counterintuitive—find a nutritionally based fitness program offered by a seasoned trainer that would come to my office in the middle of my busy day. Kevin Brown, CEO of Visionary Trainers, had such a fitness program that could accommodate my needs.

At the time I began working with Visionary Trainers, I weighed nearly 250 pounds and felt tired and mentally drained throughout most of the day. Kevin Brown met with me and designed a fitness program that included the following: Advice on healthful meal portions of proteins, carbohydrates and dairy products; Nutritional advice on vitamin and mineral supplements with high bioavailability; A strength training regimen; and routine aerobic exercises.

After seven weeks of training with Visionary Trainers, following their healthful meal plan, and using recommended nutritional supplements from New Vision, I have lost approximately sixteen pounds, gained muscle mass, and most importantly doubled my energy level. I now feel physically strong and mentally alert as I go through a typical 100-hour work week. The overall improvement in the quality of my physical and mental state has moved me to become part of the team at Visionary Trainers. As Chief Medical Officer (CMO) for Visionary Trainers, I believe I can help other physicians understand and articulate the benefits of a balanced fitness approach to their patients. I look forward to providing medical oversight to Visionary Trainers and working within the medical community on a nutrition and fitness program that I know can make a difference.

Woody Jackson, MD

Drug free and happy together

Absolutely everything Kevin Brown told my husband and I could happen if we followed his recommended way of eating, supplements, and exercise did happen in a very short period of time. We followed Kevin's recommendations, to a lesser and now greater degree, for about six weeks. We have lost weight, were relieved of chronic pain, no longer require certain medications, have more stable moods, less stress, an improved life, and in many ways an improved relationship. We experienced some of these results right away and saw all of them in about four weeks. We did not follow the program precisely but we did commit to it long term. Our goal was simply to lose some weight, but we have seen much more pervasive and profound effects. We highly recommend that you give it serious consideration.

Dean and I are by nature skeptical. We are both in high-pressure competitive industries and not inclined to trust people or feel good programs that will "change your life." However, a very dear friend had asked me to join her to hear Kevin Brown speak about nutrition and lifestyle. She told me Kevin had a great message that I needed to hear because it would revolutionize they way I thought about nutrition, and of course, it would "change my life." I admired her enthusiasm but was sure it would take a lot more than an hour lecture to revolutionize anything about me. I am forty-six years of age and have been reading diet books, going on and off diets, joining and quitting gyms, staying at health spas, researching nutrition and reading self help books for at least thirty of those years. I wasn't expecting anything new or anything that I would or could follow for more than a week.

Remarkably, what I heard was a very new message about a very old and common-sense way of eating and living that was brilliant in its simplicity. Kevin Brown suggested that we eat the way healthy societies have been eating for at least as long as those habits had been recorded. He recommended we use common sense and stop eating artificial synthetic food. Eat fats, protein and limited carbohydrates from raw milk products, eggs and grass-fed animals. Eat fruits and vegetables in season that are grown locally and without pesticides, and eat bone-based soups. Don't wash the salts and nutrients from your system through the excessive drinking of water. Eat two or at most three meals a day and exercise. Kevin explained that our modern foods are loaded with MSG and chemicals, which set up a craving for more food and keep society fat. He implored the group to open our eyes and take an honest look at the degree to which we have succumbed to food industry marketing.

I was impressed and signed up to have Kevin come to our home for an hour session so that my husband could hear Kevin's program. Dean was not receptive even a little to the idea—but he agreed. Both my husband and I are were overweight and becoming unhealthier. We had talked for over a year about doing something about it but were too tired to ever take action. Our eating habits and lack of exercise affected the way we felt physically, our moods, and the amount of medications we required. At forty-two my husband was already pre-diabetic, on high blood pressure medications, and on non-narcotic pain killers that he required daily to alleviate chronic pain associated with two back surgeries. These medications were required just to allow him to get out of bed in the morning and move with some flexibility. All of these conditions were aggravated by the extra weight. I had gained twenty pounds since we were married and was at least twenty-five pounds overweight. I was on low doses of anti-depressants, which I thought I should no longer need but couldn't seem to cut out. I had been trying to wean myself off of them for a year, with my doctor's knowledge, after taking them for nearly ten years. We felt bad, and we were beginning to look bad. We had all the side effects of unhealthy living from lack of energy to mood swings to depression. So we listened to Kevin's message, and we heard it. He weighed us, and he told us to set goals and to make a commitment. My husband was at 303 pounds with an initial goal of losing 50 pounds in eight months. I was at 144 with a goal of 25 pounds in three and half months. We decided to commit to this regardless of our skepticism. I believe it was the fact that this was a program that made sense and included foods we liked to eat.

We found local farms on line and we started to visit them, buying all of our raw milk products, eggs and grass-raised meat products locally as Kevin had taught. We began taking cod liver oil, a mineral supplement and Xango daily. We got rid of the fake food in our home. Still we didn't dive in all at once. This was right before the holidays and we did supplement Kevin's diet with the usual cookies, chocolates and rich food that abound that time of year—but we didn't want as much of these things. Something was already changing in our attitudes and preferences about food. After the holidays in January we were more consistent and by January 14, my husband, who had not yet started an exercise program, had lost seventeen pounds and I had lost seven pounds. These were not the only effects. I was able to finish with anti-depressants—not through a great conscious effort. I simply didn't need them anymore. My husband's chronic pain had diminished to the point that he has not needed to take any prescription pain medications for his back and is comfortable with less harmful over-the-counter pain relievers. This was not one of his goals or even a consideration in our new eating style. He was surprised as I was that we didn't seem to need certain meds we had previously required. Obviously we look better physically. I started with a personal trainer, and Dean is now seriously considering beginning his exercise program, so we are feeling the physical improvement. But another real bonus has been that we are mentally and emotionally better. It has been relaxing and fun to go every week to a farm together, to sit down to meals and to have committed to a type of lifestyle together.

It is a new and responsible way of life that we share, and it has had the unexpected benefit of making us even closer in our relationship.

This is not like the numerous diets I have experienced and gone off of without much thought. We now know from experience that our eating habits had been quite literally toxic. We have learned how we were meant to eat, and having experienced that sensible way of life, the cessation of food cravings, greater energy, and greater wellbeing, we simply would not consider giving that up. We encourage the most skeptical to consider Kevin Brown's approach to life and we're confident many successes will follow.

Barbara Koonz
Wayne, Pennsylvania

Muscular dystrophy improved

I want to thank you for all that you are doing for me. As you know, I've been struggling with this strange disorder called Muscular Dystrophy for over twenty years. I know that I am one of the more fortunate ones living day-to-day with this disorder; my muscle wasting more of an annoyance than completely debilitating. I've been to the best doctors in the field, each offering no real treatment or comfort from my disability. I have to say that this is the first time since my diagnosis that I've actually seen improvement, and I owe it all to you. Your belief in me, your patience and understanding, your regimen of hard work, vitamin, and mineral supplements, and your dedication has been a blessing to me. The improvement I've made, although pale in comparison to many "normal" people, is remarkable. I'm not the only one who has noticed the change. My progress has inspired many close to me to take up the challenge to change their life. The challenge is to make a commitment to eat better, to exercise regularly, and to be truly healthy.

Again, I thank you for all that you've done for me and for inspiring those around me.

Best regards, and God bless!
Yvette P. Yardley
Pennsylvania

Fasting worked for me

I want to thank Kevin Brown for all his information on the Liberation diet. I've struggled with my weight for twenty years. As my weight slowly crept past 200 pounds, I really began to lose hope. I tried so many of those fad diets out on the market, I lost track of the count. Finally, I decided I would consult a doctor on having gastric by-pass surgery. Well, the doctor said I wasn't fat enough! He said I would have to gain about another twenty pounds before I would qualify for the surgery. I thought that was one of the craziest things I'd ever heard: "Okay, let me get this straight; I need to gain twenty pounds in order to get skinny?!" My sister told me I needed to meet Kevin Brown and hear his message on the Liberation Diet. I agreed, because at this point, what did I have to lose, other than about 100 pounds? After listening to Kevin, I thought his program would be impossible, because I simply just loved to eat. His idea of fasting was the most ludicrous part to me! How could I go without a meal? I would starve!

Well, I started the diet slowly; changing my eating habits a step at a time, but I have managed to lose fifty-five pounds in just five months. And the fasting part of the diet was the thing that really helped me get past cravings and shrink my stomach, and now continues to help me keep from eating junk food. I used to be a binge and comfort eater. Now I eat when I'm hungry and don't eat when I'm not. I highly recommend the Liberation Diet for people who have struggled with their weight for years and years. And don't be afraid to fast! It really works!

Kris Messer
Concord, California

"Wow! You look Great!"

Yesterday I walked into our annual association meeting, and met a large group of people I hadn't seen in a year. "Wow! You look great!" said one. "You've gotten so skinny!" said another. What had happened in that year? I met Kevin Brown. Kevin and I have been working together for over a year now, and everything about my health has gotten better. I both look and feel better than ever before. I've gone from dreading my exercise sessions, to loving them and looking forward to them. Kevin has just the right combination of encouragement, pushing, discipline and fun. He's a great trainer. I've recommended him to all my friends. I'd recommend him to you, too.

Amanda B. Foley
Philadelphia, Pennsylvania

Help with Sheehan's syndrome

Just a note to say I am immensely pleased with my training sessions! I am extremely pleased with the results. I can comfortably wear my skirts again! I can wear jeans! I can tuck a blouse in! I have lost five pounds. Everything else has either shifted back to the right place or been converted to muscle!

Since I've had Sheehan's syndrome, I've seen many rapid, negative changes to my body. In the time I have trained with Visionary

Trainers, my muscles have awakened and are nicely sculpted! I am also stronger.

My twelve-year-old son wrestles with me—and guess who wins! I am just so pleased.

Dorothy M.
Mercerville, New Jersey

Made in the USA
Lexington, KY
09 March 2011